Char Brethin

Keep Simple Ceremonies

KEEP SIMPLE CEREMONIES

The Feminist Spiritual Community of Portland, Maine

Diane Eiker • Sapphire, Editors

ILLUSTRATED BY SYLVIA SIMS

Portland   Maine

Astarte Shell Press
P.O. Box 3648
Portland, ME 04104-3648

Grateful acknowledgement is made for permission to use the following: Harper & Row, Publishers, San Francisco, CA: excerpt from Truth or Dare, Encounters with Power, Authority and Mystery, by Starhawk, copyright 1987; Grove Press, New York, NY: excerpt from Dancing at the Edge of the World: Thoughts on Words, Women, Places, by Ursula K. LeGuin, copyright 1989; Astarte Shell Press, Portland, ME: excerpt from Vision & Struggle: Meditations on Feminist Spirituality and Politics, by Eleanor H. Haney, copyright 1990; Starhawk: the words to "Rise With The Fire" chant; Susan Savell: the words to "Simple Ceremonies" and "A Song for Jane;" Beacon Press, Boston, MA: excerpt from Gyn/Ecology: The Metaethics of Radical Feminism, by Mary Daly, copyright 1978.

LIBRARY OF CONGRESS CATALOGING-IN-PUBLICATION DATA

Keep simple ceremonies: the feminist spiritual community of
   Portland, Maine / Diane Eiker, Sapphire, editors. —
2nd. edition, expanded.
          p.   cm.
   Includes bibliographical references (pp. 186-195)
ISBN 1885349-02-5
   1. Women — Religious life   2. Rites and Ceremonies
   3. Feminism — Religious aspects.   4. Spiritual life.
   5. Seasons — Religious aspects.
I. Eiker, Diane, 1937—   II. Sapphire, 1950—
BL625.7. K44 1995
291.3'8'082 — dc 20   95-33425
                                                 CIP

Cover, book design and illustrations by Sylvia Sims, with the exception of "Celebrating the Fool," designed and illustrated by Heather Alexander, both of Portland, ME.

Printed in the USA by Bookcrafters, Fredericksburg, VA
1st. printing of Second Edition 1995

10 9 8 7 6 5 4 3 2 1

Acknowledgements

We would like to thank all those women who have been so important to the vision and realization of this book:

To the women, past and present, of the Feminist Spiritual Community for the love that created and preserved these rituals; to those who have done rituals, and to those who have made them possible by unlocking the meeting house, being brave enough to light a candle and by adding their voices to our singing circle.

To Brigit, for her courage and commitment in re-membering her own life while being a mirror to us, helping us to identify the importance of preserving our herstory.

To the Scribes ~ Charlene, Anne, Laurel, Sylvia, Gilda, Betsy, Lauren, Heather, Kristen, Mary S., Beth, Mary F., Patrice and Wendy — for helping us maintain the beauty of the handwritten word. A special thanks to Anne for developing the Resource section of this book.

To the creatures in our lives (breathing and inanimate), for their assistance and inspiration.

Finally, to our partners, Elly, Debbie and Sylvia, for their patient (and only occasionally wavering) faith in the eventual completion of this book.

Every effort has been made to accurately credit authors of songs and chants used in the rituals. If readers have information on uncredited pieces, we would be pleased to give proper credit in future editions.

Dedication

To my mother, Louise G. Walsh Stretton, and to Mrs. Audrey Hersom, my eighth grade teacher in Mechanic Falls, Maine, who said one day, "I want each of you to write a story."

Sapphire

To Lisa, Kristen and Marta who continue to challenge me to search out and speak my truth and to listen intently to theirs.

Diane

TABLE OF CONTENTS

☆ SIMPLE CEREMONIES ☆

Keep simple ceremonies
Follow the quest
Bring crystals and flowers
To the Sea mother's breast.
The earth is in ruin
And she calls for attention
Lay your hands on her body
And release all the tensions
Of hate and neglect.

I see Rainbow Woman dancing down
I see Rainbow Woman dancing down
Dancing down
Dancing down
Down and all around

The old women keep the beat
The old women keep the beat
The old women keep the beat
The old women keep the beat

And the circle seems to
meet the stars.
It shines so bright
It shines so bright

You can dance inside their grace
You can dance inside their grace
Or you can dance in your own way
You can dance in a different way

But surely you have seen the flower
of my vision on my face.
Surely you have seen
Surely you have seen the flower
Surely you have seen the flower
of my vision on my face.

Balance, balance, balance the energies
Balance, balance, balance the energies
Balance, balance, balance the energies
Of life with love.

☆ WORDS AND MUSIC BY SUSAN SAVELL ☆

Simple Ceremonies was written in response to Brooke
Medicine Eagle's vision, while in vision quest, of a healer
she named Rainbow Woman. It is a reminder that we all
need to celebrate rituals which keep us in touch with
the spirit.

x

INTRODUCTION

"A living community develops its own rituals, to celebrate life passages and ease times of transition, to connect us with the round of the changing seasons and the moon's flux, to anchor us in time. When we attempt to create community, ritual is one of our most powerful tools."

Starhawk *

This book has come out of the Ritual Book of the Feminist Spiritual Community of Portland, Maine. The Ritual Book is a hardcover volume with blank pages in which we have recorded our rituals through the first twelve years of our existence.

We have created these rituals from our varied spiritual backgrounds, to declare, honor and celebrate what has been of value to us.

The Ritual Book is precious to us — it tells our stories. In words and illustrations, it marks the building of our community — its development, its times of joy and its times of stress.

We have decided to share some of these rituals with you. They have helped so many of us to grow, laugh, cry and play. They have helped us to create a community. Through these rituals we have celebrated important passages, examined and transformed personal issues and prepared ourselves for the work of peace and justice. We know that even when we can't be sitting in the circle on Monday evening we will be brought in spirit and that we can draw the energy of Community to us wherever we are.

This book is handwritten ("scribed," as we have come to call it) in the same style as the original to honor its uniqueness and to preserve the caring and love that created it.

1

THE FEMINIST SPIRITUAL COMMUNITY

The Feminist Spiritual Community was born in June, 1980. It grew out of a course on Women and Religion at the University of Southern Maine in Portland, in which rituals were done as a class project. When the course ended, many of the women expressed a desire to create a women-only space where we could take seriously our own knowing and experiences, a space where we could explore and do ritual apart from the usual context of the patriarchy.

The small but growing group continued to meet outside the classroom, chose a name and applied to the United Church of Christ for a three-year grant for operating expenses. We received the grant. That decision by the UCC reflected an impressive amount of trust that we were doing something important since neither we nor the denomination was clear about what this group was.

During the first year we met every other week, "doing rituals and trying to figure out who we were." ** We also made several important decisions about our vision. We agreed:

~ that the circle would always be open to new women to encourage diversity and growth and to help us learn just who were our community;

~ that Mondays would be women-only space and that other activities might be open to men, children and non-members;

~ that ritual, study, support and action were all important components of the community.

The content and structure of Monday evening meetings has changed periodically, in response to the needs and interests of those participating. The size of our weekly gatherings has ranged from four to more than fifty, with an average attendance of twenty-to-thirty women.

Our perspective is primarily that of white European-American women. We range from very poor to middle class and have learned much from one another about where the "-isms" (racism, classism, sexism, agism, etc.) are in our lives.

These rituals have come from our individual traditions, needs and creativity. Out of respect for the concerns of many Native peoples at the white appropriation of their traditions, we have placed our emphasis on our own European-American experiences.

Because the personal is so often political, there are rituals in each section of the book with political dimensions. The rituals we have done have inspired us to act and have challenged us to live our visions of peace and justice. As one member observed recently, "Our rituals don't end at 9 pm on Monday nights...."

MONDAY EVENING FORMAT

We meet each Monday from 7 pm to 9 pm in Portland, Maine. The following is a synopsis of our usual evening's format.

Enfolding

When it is time to begin the meeting, all move outside the gathering space and return in twos to be greeted and hugged by the two designated enfolders, who stand at each side of the door. Participation in this welcoming is, as with all activities at Community, optional.

This practice began early in our herstory. It was used to open an evening's ritual and has been continued because of the welcoming it extends to all — to those familiar to us and to new participants as well.

Announcements

Following the enfolding, we sit in a circle (on the floor, on cushions, on low beach chairs) around an altar cloth which holds four candles and any objects central to the evening's ceremony, and make announcements.

Announcements include information about upcoming events such as concerts, political gatherings and fundraisers. We also share personal information about changes in our lives, requests for help, notices about what's new and wonderful. Announcements are not incidental to our evenings; they are an integral part of our time together.

Casting the Circle

This section consists of two parts: lighting four candles and naming ourselves.

The candles are lit for
- ~ those who are with us for the first time,
- ~ those who cannot be present but are with us in spirit,
- ~ those who are present, and
- ~ the women of our sister community in El Salvador, to whom we send financial assistance and healing energy, "con fuerza y esperanza," (with strength and hope).

Additional candles are lit if women want to honor special thoughts or needs.

The lighting of candles is followed by a naming circle. Starting with the evening's ritual leader, we go around the circle and each woman speaks her name(s) as she wishes to be known. She may also bring others to the circle in spirit, ask for whatever energy is needed and offer whatever energy she has in abundance.

Each woman, as she speaks, offers her hand to the next woman in the circle. When the circle is complete, we take a few moments to gather and circulate the energy, consider what has been asked for and offered, and to send the energy out into the world.

Ritual

This section varies each week. Those leading the evening develop a theme, working with the elements of energy movement, growth and change. The rituals often include a guided meditation, discussion, silence, movement and/or art work.

Singing

Standing, each woman joins hands with the woman <u>next</u> to the woman beside her to form a circle (see our logo at the front of the book). The songs we sing come from many places. Some are composed by women in the community, some are folk songs or chants from many different traditions, brought to us as women learn them in other places. Sometimes we know who created them, often we don't.

Many of us have discovered our voices in this closing circle, and as we stand and sway and sing, the candles on the altar cast swaying shadows on the ceiling — shadows that we like to think are the spirits of our ancestors.

Opening the Circle

In finishing our ceremonies we adapt from Starhawk: ***

By the earth that is her body
By the air that is her breath
By the fire of her bright spirit
And the waters of her living womb
The circle is open but unbroken
May the peace of the goddess go in our hearts
Merry meet and merry part
And merry meet again.
Blessed Be. Ho. Ache. ****

*   Starhawk, <u>Truth or Dare: Encounters with Power, Mystery and Authority</u> (San Francisco: Harper & Row, 1987), p. 296.

**   Feminist Spiritual Community Members' Handbook, 1988.

***   Starhawk; <u>Truth or Dare</u>, op. cit., p. 108.

****   Pronounced <u>ah-shay</u>, means power. For a discussion of <u>ache</u>, see Patrice Wynne, "Practical Wisdom: Interview with Luisah Teish," <u>The Womanspirit Sourcebook</u> (San Francisco: Harper & Row, 1988), p. 40.

Foreword to the Second Edition

Once upon a time, in a place called Maine, there was a group of women who gathered every Monday evening to do rituals to celebrate their lives — to tell their stories, to meditate, to cry and laugh together and to sing. They didn't want to forget their rituals, so they wrote them down in a book and drew beautiful pictures to decorate them.

Most of all, the women loved to sing! One of these women, Susan Savell, wrote and sang many powerful songs and she taught them to the other women. Her songs were so beautiful that a recording was made of them so women everywhere could hear them and feel their beauty. Two of the other women, Sapphire and Diane, looked at the book where others had recorded their rituals and thought how wonderful it would be if women everywhere could share its wisdom and joy. So they put the rituals in a new book that could be printed and sent anywhere there were women who would want to read it. They called the book Keep Simple Ceremonies after one of Susan's songs.

At the same time, far away, in a place called New Jersey, a woman named Gail Karger was on her spiritual journey. Along the way, she found Susan's music and loved the songs very much. She wished deep in her heart that someday she could meet Susan and the other women. She even went searching for Susan one day with her husband, Steve, and her children Harry and Miriam, when they were playing at their favorite place, a beach in Maine. But Gail couldn't find Susan.

Gail had another deep desire. She loved her children, Harry and Miriam, very much, and she and Steve also wanted to have another child. Then, in the spring, after long waiting and many disappointments, it seemed that their wish could come true. Gail was pregnant! The child within her continued to grow and to thrive. This was their miracle baby.

When it was still three months before the baby was due to be born, Gail found Keep Simple Ceremonies and brought it home with her. Here was mention of Susan Savell and the women in Maine that Susan had sung her songs with! Before she could sit down and enjoy it, however, she needed to do an errand with Steve, Harry and Miriam. While they were out, Gail suddenly became very sick and her heart stopped beating.

8

Harry, Miriam and Steve worked very quickly to get help for Gail. Rescue workers were able to start her heart again, then rushed her to the hospital. The doctors worked very quickly to take the baby from Gail's belly so that they could keep her in a place where she would be safer. She was so tiny! She only weighed one-and-a-half pounds, and her legs were only as big as Steve's finger.

That night, very worried, Steve went home from the hospital to be with Harry and Miriam. He knew that Gail was very sick, and he knew that it was difficult for a baby as tiny as theirs to live and to grow. He called his friends, Gail's church and his Temple and asked them all to pray for Gail and their miracle baby. Then Steve found the book that Gail had bought that day and read about the women in Maine. He called the women and asked them to send healing energy and prayers to Gail and to their baby.

For three Monday evenings, when the women gathered, they did healing circles for Gail and the baby, and for Steve, Harry and Miriam. Sapphire and Diane talked with Steve every week to hear how everyone was doing. Then came the sad day that Steve called to say that Gail had died.

The women mourned and knew that they had lost a friend, even if they had never met Gail. They knew, too, that they still had four other new friends — Steve, Harry, Miriam and their miracle baby who was now called Nasia (miracle of God) Ivana (God's gracious gift) Belmar (beautiful sea, the name of the rescue squad whose quick work made it possible for her to survive) Karger.

One day a short time later, Steve, Harry and Miriam (Nasia was still too tiny to leave the hospital) again visited their favorite beach in Maine, and this time they also visited their new friends, Diane and some of the other women of the Feminist Spiritual Community. Several months later Steve called to say that the exciting day had finally arrived — Nasia had come home from the hospital! She was still very tiny, and she needed lots of special attention, but they were very happy to finally have her with them.

The women were very anxious to meet Nasia, whom they thought of as their little goddessdaughter, so when she had grown a little bit stronger they invited Nasia and her father, brother and sister to come and be a part of a special ritual one Monday evening. The women told the story of how they had written their Rituals in a book and sent it out to the world, and Steve told the story of how the book had come into their home and of Gail and of how Nasia had been born. Then they all knew how they had entered into and touched each others' lives and they mourned and rejoiced and celebrated the circle that was their lives.

We offer this second edition, with its six new Rituals, in the hope that it will continue to touch others and bring us full circle always.

RITUALS

USING THIS BOOK

The book is divided into four sections—Life Cycle Rituals, Personal Milestones, Seasons of the Earth and Community.

The Life Cycle rituals follow nature's time in a woman's life, from birth through growth and aging to death.

The Personal Milestone rituals honor times of change, whether chosen or unchosen.

New to this edition, the Seasonal rituals celebrate the four cross-quarter days in the Celtic calendar, as well as the high holiday honoring the goddess April Foola.

The Community rituals bring together our spirituality, politics and our day-to-day lives. One member recently said that being in community "lets me bring together all the parts of my life into one whole."

These rituals are not intended to be used verbatim, but as templates for envisioning and revisioning the aspects of our lives that we need and wish to honor, mourn and celebrate.

Ritual Format

There are several elements common to all the rituals in this book. Other elements are individual to each ritual and are described when used or are noted in the glossary. For more complete descriptions of Casting the Circle, Singing and Opening the Circle as used at the Feminist Spiritual Community, see the "Monday Evening Format" in the Introduction.

Materials

To aid in preparation for the ritual, this section in each ritual contains a list of what materials will be needed.

Casting the Circle

This can be any activity designed to define the boundaries of what will be considered sacred space during the ritual. The circle is cast at the beginning of a gathering and opened at the end.

Introducing the Ritual

This section includes information to be shared with those participating in the ritual. We encourage you to add any other information that is important to you.

Meditation

Rituals frequently include a guided meditation.
Each meditation begins with the instructions "Relax, etc. . . . ." Establishing relaxation is an important aspect of beginning a guided meditation. Some of the elements of relaxation are: slow, even breathing; imaging the intake of healing energy and the release of tensions and worries; the establishing of ritual space as a place of safety. Take time to establish this relaxation before moving into the body of the meditation so that those listening will be more present, less distracted, and will get more out of the

journey. We encourage you to create your own relaxation instructions. For more information on relaxation and meditations see _Mother Wit_ by Diane Mariechild and _Casting the Circle_ by Diane Stein in the Resource list.

Singing

Singing songs that empower you is a wonderful way to ground yourselves and take some of the energy of the evening home with you.

Opening the Circle

It is important to bring your ritual to a definite close and to release the energy you have gathered.

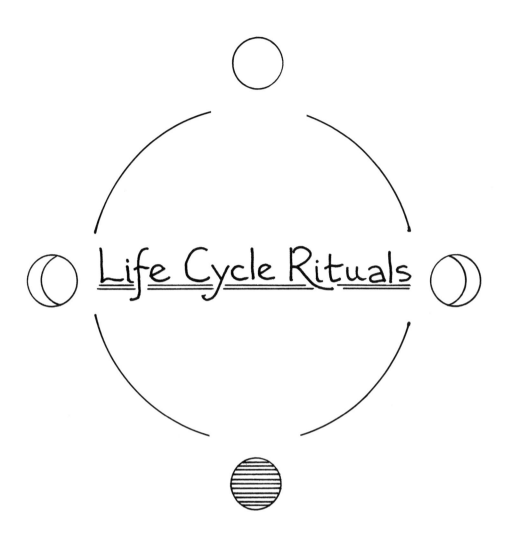

BABY BLESSING

This is a short, very simple ceremony, created for babies and their mothers to offer protection and wisdom

MATERIALS

Barley
Salt
Container of Moonwater (see glossary)

CASTING THE CIRCLE

CEREMONY

Invite the new mothers to stand with their babies in the center of the room.

All other mothers form a circle around them. One of the mothers sprinkles barley around those in the center that they may never want from hunger of the body or of the soul.

Grandmothers form another circle. One of them sprinkles salt around the circle of mothers and babies for the wisdom of the earth.

All others form a third circle and sprinkle moonwater, offering the gift of sisterhood.

SINGING

Songs,

especially lullabies,

are offered to the new babies

and their mothers.

OPENING THE CIRCLE

21

MENARCHE

Many of us have specific, often less than fond, memories of when we began our menses. This ritual was designed because our culture so often prefers silence (or misinformation) at times when knowledge of our bodies' changes should be freely and lovingly taught. It celebrates a young woman's beginning her menses. This ritual honors the passage of one young woman but can be adapted if there is more than one celebrant.

Materials

  Altarcloth of moonphases (or other altar cloth)
  Moon imagery for altar — pictures, jewelry, other art
  Flowers — red and white
  Bowl of red earth, garnet sand or ochre — as available
  Bowl of moonwater (see glossary)
  Candles — red, white and black
  Length of red ribbon — at least ½ yard for each woman
  Scissors

Casting The Circle

In addition to the usual candles, light three for the three traditional aspects of the goddess: white for the maiden (new, fresh, innocent, beginning); red for the mother (creative, generative, nurturing); black for the crone (wise, self-knowing).

As you name yourselves, ask each woman to bring someone who embodies maiden energy.

Introducing The Ritual

We have gathered here with a very special purpose. As a community of women, we have come to acknowledge, affirm and honor our life transitions. Our lives bring many changes and opportunities to celebrate beginnings, endings and new learnings.

There are three phases of a woman's bleeding: ovulation and the filling of the womb; active bleeding; cessation of bleeding, with a period of rest. While these phases do not often coincide exactly with the moon's phases, they do correspond to the waxing, fullness and waning of the moon.

We are here to celebrate the beginnings of womanhood and ending of childhood that firstblood brings. We celebrate a child-becoming-woman who is here to be welcomed into our circle.

 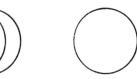 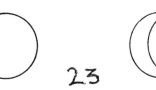  

Invocation to The Four Directions and the Center

 Spirit of the East, of new moon and morning star; Spirit of Spring and new beginnings, where new life and creative projects are born into being;

Be with us now.

 Spirit of the South, of noon sun, volcano fire and lava flow; spirit of the sacred blood of life;

Be with us now.

 Spirit of the West, of water and emotions; Spirit of the moon tides in our bodies and in our spirits;

Be with us now.

 Spirit of the North; of dreams, visions and inner wisdom; spirit which cradles and protects us as we go within, to the darkness;

Be with us now.

 Spirit of the Center, of balancing our many aspects; spirit of peace and trust in our inner being; spirit of balance between our outer and inner lives;

Be with us now.

Meditation

Relax, etc. . . . .

Notice how your body is supported by the floor. As your muscles continue to release their tension, your thoughts flow like water in a brook, bubbling and gurgling over and around the rocks, branches and pebbles, downward, flowing, away. . . .

You follow the brook as it widens, deepens, narrows. It changes, sometimes gently, sometimes suddenly. . . . As you continue to follow this brook-becoming-stream, notice the water music, the song it sings as you are flowing . . . together . . . downward. It sings your name . . . it chants and repeats your name in rhythms and rounds, as together you flow . . . as together . . . flowing . . . your name resounds. The stream meanders and bends as it flows and widens and deepens.

Your thoughts flow and deepen as you think of your mother . . . or your mother as she might have been, as she thinks of her mother . . . your grandmother. Your mother, standing beside you, holding your hand, turns and extends her other hand to your grandmother, humming and chanting your name as the water flows, deepening and growing wider.

You see them, and as you are watching them your grandmother turns and extends her hand to _her_ mother, who speaks your name, as the water flows deeply, widening. She turns and reaches her hand out to _her_ mother, who takes the hand of _her_ mother ... flowing and sounding your name, softly, gently, lovingly and clearly.

Back and onward, deeply, softly surging, flowing downward as your foremothers continue to reach back to their foremothers, as the stream widens to a river, and the river widens, finally, into the sea.

(Pause one minute)

You wash in the seawater and then lie on the warm, clean sand, aware of the peacefulness, the way you feel lovingly known in this place. As you rest here you drift dreamily, hearing the gentle waves, smelling the salt air as it whispers your name.

You see a woman coming toward you. She comes and sits next to you. She looks familiar, yet different and unfamiliar. She says to you:

"I am the spirit of your foremothers, from the depths of time. I am empowered by all of them to speak to

26

you today. They ask me to tell you of our love for you. They want you to know how we share in your hopes and dreams. We support you in your trials and challenges. We celebrate your growth and your life. We bless your heart, your passionate fire and your truth. We honor your will and determination, and we honor your voice, as you express yourself and communicate with others in this life. We, the many, many women before you, offer the gift of wisdom, insight and vision available to you whenever you look within.

"We celebrate the strength, sensuality, vitality and beauty of your body. As you love and care for it respectfully, it will serve you well. Honor your rhythms and cycles - in these you are connected with all women of all time, even as you are uniquely and newly yourself. Know that your precious menstrual blood is sacred to us, as it represents the life force, the elemental source and cycle of birth, life, death and birth.

"Seek balance and appreciation for all of your being, allowing expression of your inner and outer awareness, receiving and giving, stillness and action, creating outwardly, renewing within, in rest, work and play. Blossom in every way, expressing the perfect, whole, powerful beauty of your being a woman in your chosen time.

27

"Know that you are, through us, connected to the beginning, to the Goddess, the source of life. She lives as you live, sees as you see, loves as you love, guides, protects and holds you. She, too, knows your name."

(Pause one minute)

Your foremother tells you that she must return to her time, as you must to yours. You ask her name and she tells you. You know that you will see her again when you go within and ask for her. She will guide and help you all of your life, as you wish.

You embrace her healing presence and again sense the flow of the river, as your many foremothers wave goodbye to you for now. You feel the flow of the stream, the flow of the brook, you hear your name spoken softly as you return, coming gently back to this place and time ... back to this room ... You feel the floor beneath you, supporting your body.... When you are ready, gently and slowly open your eyes and softly speak your name.

Discussion (large or small group)

Share your thoughts and images from the meditation — memories or anticipations of young womanhood, growing up, sexuality and learning.

Moonwater Blessing

Each woman sits before the young woman and offers a blessing with the moonwater.

Youngwoman Speaks

The young woman being honored shares a few words on how she feels about beginning this passage.

Ribbon

One end of the length of ribbon is started around the circle, with the hands of each woman retaining a light hold as the ribbon slides through her fingers until all are holding a portion of the ribbon.

Someone says:

"This ribbon is to remind us of our common and sacred connection with one another, with all women, with our foremothers, the Goddess and the Earth."

All hold the ribbon for a moment, visualizing these connections, and then scissors are passed so that each woman can keep her length as a gift.

Singing

Opening The Circle

Feasting

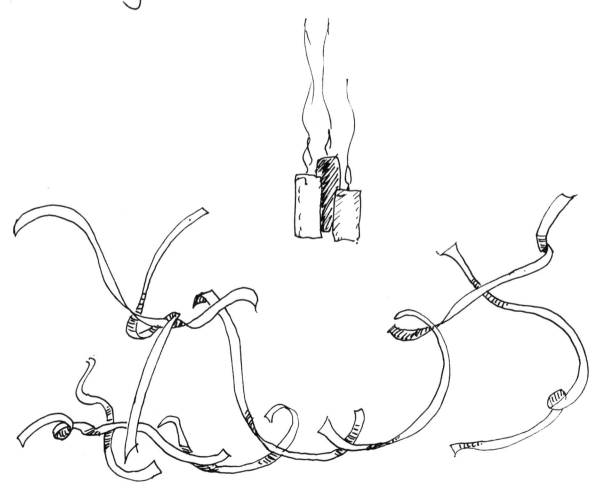

THIS RITUAL WAS DESIGNED BY WILLOW, AN FSC MEMBER, TO CELEBRATE "... THE JOY AND RICHNESS OF MY LIFE NOW, AND TO CONTRADICT THE NEGATIVE CONNOTATIONS ASSOCIATED WITH THIS PASSAGE IN OUR CULTURE."

MATERIALS

BIRTHDAY CANDLE
FOUR CANDLES FOR DECADES
BOWL OF MOONWATER (SEE GLOSSARY) OR SALTWATER
HAND MIRROR

CASTING THE CIRCLE

BESIDES THE USUAL CANDLES, AN EXTRA CANDLE IS LIT FOR/BY THE WOMAN CELEBRATING HER BIRTHDAY.

INTRODUCING THE RITUAL

IN EUROPEAN TRADITIONS, THE GODDESS AS MOON REPRESENTS THE EVER-CHANGING CYCLES OF ENERGY IN OUR WOMAN-BODIES. THE CRESCENT, FULL AND DECRESCENT MOON HAVE REPRESENTED THE THREE MAJOR ASPECTS OF A WOMAN'S LIFE — THE MAID, MOTHER AND CRONE.

COLORS OF THE MOON GODDESS ARE RED, FOR THE MENSTRUAL TIDES OF HER DAUGHTERS, AND GREEN FOR THE GROWTH SHE NURTURES. GODDESSES OF THE FULL MOON ARE HATHOR, EGYPTIAN GODDESS OF LOVE AND JOY; AND YEMAYA, CENTRAL AND SOUTH AMERICAN AND AFRICAN OCEAN MOTHER.

In celebrating this fortieth birthday, we celebrate the mother / lover / creator aspect of the goddess — the woman at the height of her choices, her growth, her personal power; the woman full of passion for life — the sensual, creative, powerful, nurturing woman who is a source of life to herself as well as to others.

Invocation

GODDESS OF THE NIGHTTIME SKY
    SOURCE OF LIFE
        HOLDER OF SENSUALITY AND LOVE
SWELLING TO FULLNESS, YOU EMBRACE CREATIVITY
WITHDRAWING TO DARKNESS, YOU BRING SILENCE
        AND THE SEEKING OF INNER KNOWLEDGE
SEND US YOUR MOONPATH TO GUIDE US INTO YOUR LIGHT
BE WITH US NOW

Decade Candles

The birthday woman lights a candle for each decade she has lived and talks about what has been important for her in each period. Others are invited to think about (but not necessarily share) what was important for them in those years.

Meditation

Relax, etc...

You are going on a journey ... a journey to the edge of the ocean ... to the edge of the ocean where the sands of the beach still hold a hint of warmth from the day's sun ...

SMELL THE SCENT OF THE SEA CARRIED ON THE WARM TWILIGHT
BREEZE, AS THE STARS BRIGHTEN IN THE DARKENING SKY . . .

YOU STAND ON THE BEACH AND LOOK OFF ACROSS THE WATER
TO WHERE THE MOON, IN ALL HER ROUND FULLNESS, HAS JUST RISEN
DIRECTLY BEFORE YOU. PART OF HER STILL TOUCHES THE WATER. SHE
LOOKS ALMOST LARGE ENOUGH AND CLOSE ENOUGH TO TOUCH. YOU
FEEL THE GLOW OF HER LIGHT LIKE A SMILE UPON YOU.

THE LIGHT FROM THE MOON CASTS A YELLOW PATH ON THE
WATER . . . A PATH THAT LEADS DIRECTLY TO WHERE YOU STAND ON
THE BEACH. THE PATH STOPS AT YOUR FEET, AND AS YOUR EYE FOLLOWS
IT BACK TO THE MOON'S ROUND FULLNESS, YOU HEAR A VOICE SAY:
"COME . . . WALK ON THE MOON PATH . . . CROSS THE WATER ON THE
RIBBON OF LIGHT . . . I AM THE GODDESS OF THE MOON . . .
COME, BE WITH ME . . .

YOU STEP ON THE PATH OF LIGHT WITH NO FEAR . . . AND YOU TRAVEL
ACROSS THE WATER TO THE MOON . . . TO WHERE SHE JUST TOUCHES THE
WAVES . . .

(PAUSE 15 SECONDS)

YOU STEP INTO THE SOFT LIGHT OF THE MOON AND FIND THE
GODDESS WAITING FOR YOU . . . THE GODDESS WHO IS MOTHER . . .
LOVER . . . FULL OF LIFE AND POWER . . . THE GODDESS WHO IS
SENSUAL . . . CREATIVE . . . NURTURING . . . FEELING . . .
THE GODDESS WHO IS A SOURCE OF LIFE TO HERSELF AS WELL AS TO
OTHERS . . . AND YOU ARE NOT IN THE LEAST SURPRISED TO FIND THAT
HER FACE BECOMES YOUR OWN . . . THAT SHE IS YOU IN YOUR MOTHER
ASPECT, AND THAT YOU ARE SHE . . .

SHE TAKES YOU BY THE HAND AND YOU WALK TOGETHER IN THE
WARM, GLOWING NIGHT . . . AND YOU TALK . . .

(PAUSE 15 SECONDS)

33

AFTER A WHILE YOU SIT, AND SHE GATHERS HANDFULS OF THE WARM, GLOWING LIGHT AND BATHES YOU IN IT . . . LETS IT RUN DOWN OVER YOU LIKE WARM HONEY . . . YOU FEEL THE LIGHT SEEP INTO YOU . . . INTO EVERY PART OF YOU . . . AND YOU FEEL INFUSED WITH YOUR OWN FULL POWER . . .

(PAUSE 30 SECONDS)

SHE SAYS THAT HER GIFT TO YOU IS THE GIFT OF CREATIVITY, AND THAT YOU WILL BE ABLE TO EXPERIENCE YOUR SENSUAL, SEXUAL BEING WHENEVER YOU CHOOSE . . . EXPERIENCE YOURSELF NOW AS MOTHER AND LOVER OF YOUR OWN LIFE . . .

(PAUSE 30 SECONDS — 1 MINUTE)

YOU FEEL, AFTER A WHILE, THAT IT'S TIME TO RETURN . . . YOU STAND AND TURN BACK TOWARD THE BEACH. THE GODDESS WHO IS YOURSELF SAYS: "COME BE WITH ME ANYTIME . . . I AM ALWAYS HERE . . . ON THE OTHER SIDE OF THE MOONPATH . . . AND I AM ALSO ALWAYS WITHIN YOU . . . "

SHE ENFOLDS YOU AND THEN YOU TURN AND STEP OUT OF THE WARM, GLOWING LIGHT . . . ONTO THE MOONPATH . . . . YOU WALK BACK ACROSS THE GLIMMERING WATER TO THE BEACH, WHERE YOU STAND FOR A WHILE AND WATCH THE FULL MOON RISE HIGHER AND HIGHER INTO THE NIGHTTIME SKY . . . BATHED IN HER LIGHT, FEELING HER FULLNESS WITHIN YOU . . .

AND WHEN YOU ARE READY . . . COME BACK TO THIS CIRCLE . . . TO THESE WOMEN . . . AND VERY SLOWLY OPEN YOUR EYES . . .

SELF BLESSING

THE BOWL OF MOONWATER / SALTWATER IS PASSED AROUND THE

CIRCLE. EACH WOMAN WHO WANTS TO SPEAKS BRIEFLY OF HOW SHE IS NOW EXPERIENCING THE FULLNESS OF THE MOTHER/LOVER IN HER LIFE. SHE THEN BLESSES HERSELF WITH THE WATER WHILE LOOKING INTO THE MIRROR, SAYING " (NAME) , THOU ART GODDESS."

CLOSING

STAND AND JOIN HANDS, SINGING "HAPPY BIRTHDAY" IN ANY VERSIONS YOU KNOW AND "FULL MOONLIGHT DANCE".*

SINGING

OPENING THE CIRCLE

* WRITTEN BY KAREN BETH, THIS SONG CAN BE FOUND ON THE LIBANA CASSETTE A CIRCLE IS CAST; SPINNING RECORDS; P.O. BOX 530, CAMBRIDGE, MA 02140

MY BODY AS ART

This ritual was done at FSC in June of 1994, by two women who had been participating in a group focusing on body issues. They wanted to share with the rest of the group what they had learned about themselves.

MATERIALS

Music to be played during meditation
Tape player

CASTING THE CIRCLE

INTRODUCING THE RITUAL

This ritual is about body image — our images of ourselves and society's images of us. In doing this work, we have become more aware of the messages we receive about how our bodies "should" look and behave. We have been exploring our feelings about these expectations as well as our feelings about what looks good and feels good to us. We bring this work here because community is about sharing our own personal struggles and insights.

We will move, in this ritual, from encouraging you to relax into who you are within your body, through an awareness of how you see yourself, into an appreciation of your own innate physical beauty.

PUTTING AT EASE

Reading: "Ode to My Hips," from <u>Some Body to Love</u>.＊
This is a humorous poem about taking joy and
claiming power in your own body. If this book is
not available to you, find a piece to substitute
which would give a similar flavor.

MOVING INTO AWARENESS

Grounding Excercise

Stand in a circle, feet shoulder width apart. Plant
your feet firmly on the floor and bounce gently, bending
your knees slightly; feel your center of gravity shift
down to your feet. Take a deep breath — pull the air
down into your toes. Relax your shoulders . . . let your
arms hang at your sides. Relax your neck and let your
head drop forward onto your chest. Let it roll clockwise
around your neck . . . all the way around . . . now
once more around . . . until it returns to your chest.
Now reverse the motion and let your head roll in the
opposite direction . . . all the way around . . . and once
more around.
　Now turn to the right and begin to walk slowly and
silently, following a circular path, around the room. Keep
your knees bent . . . step firmly into each step . . . keep
your center of gravity in your feet. Keep your eyes
down . . . forget that there are other people in the room.
Turn off your intellect . . . breathe and walk.

(walk 1 minute)

Now begin to speed up... keep your knees bent... keep your center of gravity low... remember to breathe.

(walk 3-5 minutes)

Now begin to slow down... keep your eyes down... keep your knees bent. Slow down until you return to your place in the circle. Stand for a moment, feeling your connection to the earth, then sit, ready for the next exercise.

Big and Small Exercise * *

In ancient Tahiti, the queens were encouraged to be fat. Being big was a sign of health and power. In our culture women are rewarded for being thin and small. Without muscles. Weak. It is still a matter of social awkwardness for the woman in a heterosexual couple to be taller than the man. The symbolic hierarchy is upset.

This exercise gives you a chance to experiment with feelings about your size. You will imagine yourself growing and shrinking, like Alice with her mushrooms, and notice how you feel being different sizes.

Now imagine you are getting slightly thinner and smaller. How does it feel? Imagine that someone you know is in the room. This is a person who is sometimes threatening to you. Let yourself shrink even more until you are very tiny compared to that person. How do you feel in relation to him or her? What is happening in your body right now....? How does it feel?

Now imagine that you have the power to expand yourself, so that you are proportionately growing broader and taller. Pay attention to your attitude toward the other person as you get larger. At which size do you feel most comfortable with this person? Is it when you are tiny, when you are nearly as large as they, when you two are equal in size, or when you are bigger?

38

Keep expanding and growing. What is happening inside your body now? How does it feel? Let yourself blow up like a balloon, so that you are huge in the room and the other person is proportionately very tiny. How do you feel now?

Now let yourself come back to your usual size. Let yourself remember how your body felt as you shrank and as you expanded. What did your muscles do? What else did you feel?

Relax again, and go inside your body. Now be aware of a layer of energy that surrounds your body. This energy is also a part of your body and forms an outer protective boundary for you. Make this energy shield expand now to double its former size. Let yourself relax in this aura, knowing that no one can come inside unless you want them to.

Be with your body now, and when you are ready, open your eyes and be a part of the circle.

DISCUSSION

Talk about images and/or feelings that came up in the exercises, what your body image is or has been or could be, what it feels like to be big or small in relation to others.

APPRECIATION

Reading: Excerpt from The Girl Who Swallowed The Moon * * * This excerpt tells of a young woman's appreciation of every part of her body and of her new awareness of her sensual connections to the earth, the air and the nighttime sky.

39

Meditation (with music to move by) * * * *

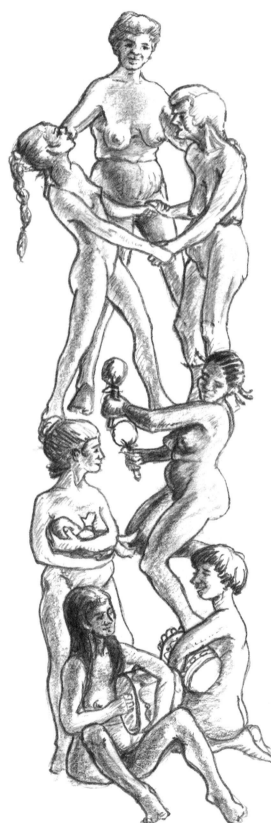

HOW AM I ART

My body has always been art
But I see in new ways.

My eyes clear, penetrating
Seeking truth.
My mouth that laughs, speaks
sometimes with wisdom, screams
sometimes in rage.

My head lined with age and
seasons held with pride and
courage.
My body has always been art
and I see in new ways.

My heart open and loving.
My breasts pulled lower with each act
   of nurturing and pleasure.
My solar plexus, my will
that gives me discipline and
drive.

My body has always been art
and I see in new ways.
My belly, my source of power
source of creativity.

My body has always been art
and I see in new ways.

My hands my large delicate
red arthritic rubbed raw
strong hands

40

My hands make magic
cast spells and circles.
My hands channel healing
calmness tenderness
caress cool weave webs.

My hands make sculpture
clay carve cut construct
never tire, always flashing.
My hands draw, write,
color, create illusions
make magic.
My hands that do the roughest
crudest
work clean chop
lift carry.
My hands that do the most
delicate most precise work
surgical microscopic measuring.
My hands clean pet love
heal and always make magic.

My fire that begins a child.
My fire that begins my art,
My fire my magic my center my
source is in my belly the
cauldron called womb.

My body has always been art
and I see in new ways.

My vulva, clitoris, labia.
My sexuality my womanhood.

My flow my tide my menses.
The redness of my blood
dark purple red sienna

41

the many-colored flow tied
to the moon and to the earth.
My body has always been art
and I see in new ways.
My shoulders that carry
many burdens. Full of strength.
My back slow to tire. Full
of strength.
My arms graceful, eloquent
and strong.

My body has always been art
and I see in new ways.
Thighs large sturdy able to lift heavy burdens,
maintain center of gravity.
My feet that carry me on my path. That climb
and explore.
My feet that root me to the earth and bring me
energy through her.

My body has always been art
and I see in new ways.

Written by Gina Kelley

SONG

"Yes To Life!" * * * * *

SINGING

OPENING THE CIRCLE

42

* Lesléa Newman, "Ode to my hips," from <u>Some Body to Love: A Guide to Loving the Body You Have</u>, p. 40, (Chicago: Third Side Press, 1991).

** Anne Kent Rush, <u>Getting Clear: Body Work For Women</u>, p. 69, adapted from "The Little Woman," exercise. (Co-published by New York, NY: Random House and Berkeley, CA: The Bookworks, 1973).

*** Melanie Gideon, <u>The Girl Who Swallowed The Moon</u>, pp 12-14, Section 2, (Portland, ME: Astarte Shell Press, 1995).

**** We suggest something from Gabrielle Roth's <u>Ritual: Rituals of Remembrance for a Forgotten Earth</u>, Raven Recording, P.O. Box 2034, Red Bank, NJ, 07701.

***** Written by Karen Howe, recorded by Heather Bishop on <u>Old, New, Borrowed, Blue</u>, Mother-of-Pearl Records, Inc., 1992, Woodmore, Manitoba, R0A 2M0.

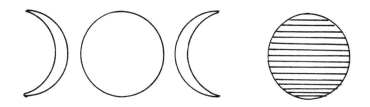

MENOPAUSE

This ritual celebrates the passage from Mother to Crone. It is designed for one or more women celebrating her (their) change with a group of other women — maidens, mothers and crones.

MATERIALS

Six candles — colors of the rainbow
Gate — an archway, tall enough for a woman to pass through
Two items of ritual clothing — a garment, jewelry, a shawl, scarf, shoes, a hat, etc. — one to be worn by the celebrant before her passage through the gate and the other after. The celebrant should be wearing the first garment at the beginning of the ritual
Music — for meditation — we suggest Kay Gardner's "A Rainbow Path"*

CASTING THE CIRCLE

INTRODUCING THE RITUAL

Menopause is much more than a cessation of fertility — much more than the loss of the ability to give birth to another being.

It is a time when the blood that has been available for giving life to others is now being kept within to nurture oneself.

Menopause means that we can let go of the

mother/creator energy in our lives. We can let go of the monthly cycle that joins us to each other and to nature. We can let go of the cramping and the pain.

Menopause is an opportunity to take on a new freedom. In "keeping our wise blood inside"** we have both a biological source for a new energy and a symbol of a new life. We experience increased energy, a feeling of power and a new sense of self that focuses more on meeting our own individual needs than on meeting the needs of others.

Ursula K. LeGuin said about menopause, "Loss of fertility ... does entail a change .... The woman who is willing to make that change must become pregnant with herself, at last. She must bear herself, her third self, her old age ...."***

While aging and the changes in our bodies are not processes we can control, the active, conscious shift from one predominant energy to another is a choice.

We are gathered here to celebrate the passage of this woman (these women) as she moves into her time of wisdom.

INVOCATION

The six rainbow candles are lit one-by-one, either by the woman celebrating her passage or by a facilitator. If there is more than one celebrant, they can share the lighting.

"We come to celebrate my passage to menopause. I light these candles for my journey:

"I light this RED candle to honor the red river of life which runs within me.
"I light this ORANGE candle to celebrate the fire and creation that dance within me.
"I light this YELLOW candle for the powers of the

mind, for my intellect, which gains wisdom with the passage of time,.

"I light this GREEN candle for growth, for the things that I have planted on earth and for all that I have nurtured.

"I light this BLUE candle for all the emotions that I have experienced, for the joy and sorrow, knowing that they are part of the great Wheel of Life, and that to know them both is the only way to experience full womanhood.

"I light this PURPLE candle for my spirituality, which never ceases, but rather increases as I travel my journey."

MEDITATION

This is a meditation in which women move or dance rather than sit or lie still. It helps each woman gather her energy for her part in the passage.

All stand (or sit, if needed) in a circle. Begin music.

Stand comfortably, take a deep breath, pulling it deep into your lungs, down into your belly, down your legs into your feet. Exhale slowly, letting any tension you find in these areas relax as you breathe out.

Take another deep breath, letting the energy flow down your arms, down to your fingertips, letting any tightness in your arms relax as you exhale.

Continuing to breathe deeply, bend your knees ... flex the muscles in your arms ... your legs ... your shoulders ... Move around a little to loosen up the joints ... Turn your head side-to-side. Let it fall gently forward, then rotate it around to ease any tightness ...

Breathe deeply...

Be aware of your body, of your own energy...
Be aware of what phase of your life you are living and
of what you most enjoy about this time of your life...

Are you a maiden — celebrating your developing
body... your discoveries of the world... making
friends...?

Are you a mother — celebrating your sensual,
creative self... your full woman's body... your
choices...?

Are you a crone — celebrating your growing
wisdom... your self-nurturance... your
satisfaction at surviving...?

Let your face relax and smile as you think of
what is most exciting, most enjoyable about being who
you are... about being the age you are...

What is best in your life now? What would convince
you to stay right here where you are, in this phase of
your life?

Take a deep breath and let yourself smile as you
think of this time in your life...

(pause)

Breath deeply... move your body... bend your
knees... gently flex your muscles... be aware of
yourself...

And when you are ready, slowly return to this
circle and open your eyes...

PASSAGE

The gate is set in the center of the room. Maidens and mothers stand on one side of the gate and crones stand on the other. The celebrant stands at the gateway.

In the meditation, women gained insights into who they are right now. Mothers and maidens call now to the celebrant, telling her of the best aspects of their lives, telling her she should stay with them and not undertake this passage. They laugh, plead, cajole. They reach out to her.

The crones do the same from the other side of the gate— calling their sister to join them, telling her what they most love about who they are— what cronehood has to offer. They, too reach out to her.

When the woman is ready to make her passage, she hands the garment symbolizing her letting go to the maidens and mothers and passes beneath the archway to join the crones, who welcome her with cheers, hugs and congratulations. A choice has been made and acted upon. They offer her a garment to symbolize what she is taking on.

The crones offer songs, readings, words of wisdom to the woman.

The celebrant talks to all about her passage.

Then all join hands around the archway and sing.

SINGING

OPENING THE CIRCLE

* Produced by Ladyslipper, Inc., PO Box 3124, Durham, NC 27705, 1984
** Lucia Francia, <u>Dragontime: Magic and Mystery of Menstruation</u> (Woodstock, NY: Ash Tree Publishing, 1991), p. 124
*** Ursula K. LeGuin, "The Space Crone," from <u>Dancing At the Edge of the World: Thoughts on Words, Women, Places</u>, (New York, NY: Grove Press, 1989) p. 5

CRONING CEREMONY

This has become one of the most popular rituals celebrated at FSC. Women have spoken of coming back after an absence, or of deciding to continue membership, solely on the power they felt in this ceremony. It has been celebrated, with few changes, more than any other in our herstory.

In our community the croning ceremony traditionally has been planned for the new crones by those who have already become crones, but you may wish to include the new crones in this process.

ALTAR AND MATERIALS

Candle for the crones
Crystals ~ amethyst or other crystal, one for each
    woman being "croned"
Crone jewel ~ one special crystal to be placed on
    the altar each time this ritual is done ~ a
    continuing symbol of the crone's wisdom
Stole ~ one for each woman, as a symbol of her
    passage*
Altar cloth ~ bright purple, the color of wisdom
Pictures ~ of crones important to those attending

BIRTHING CANAL (see glossary)

CASTING THE CIRCLE

Besides the usual candles, light the crone candle
    and ask each woman to bring a crone.

Introducing the Ritual
Why We Celebrate the Crone

The Feminist Spiritual Community has defined a crone as any woman who is fifty-six years of age or older, and who has gone through menopause. By the age of fifty-six, Saturn, the teaching planet, has returned twice in a woman's life. Sometimes a woman may identify herself as a crone before one or both of these guidelines is reached. Because FSC prefers guidelines to rules, this is perfectly acceptable.

We are here to celebrate the attainment of the age of wisdom in a woman's life. Our patriarchal society does not recognize crones as the wise, powerful older women that they are.

In such a society women are seen as belonging only in supporting and subservient roles, where their usefulness is defined by their physiological functions in sex, reproduction and mothering. In such a society crones are considered to be old, useless and dysfunctional.

Through a feminist tradition, we bring to the croning ceremony a new appreciation of women of all ages.

In celebrating crones, we honor:

Bodily changes ~ we see menopause not only as an ending, but also as a beginning of a new freedom.

Changing relationships ~ perceptions of ourselves and others undergo tremendous changes, especially our perceptions of our children, our plans and ambitions, our sense of the future and of our own mortality.

Experience ~ we respect long life, stories of pain and survival and the wisdom of the crone.

51

DECADE CIRCLES

The decade circles is a ritual technique created by FSC to name the major themes of a woman's life as it makes visual the aging process.

To begin the decade circles, all women are standing in one large circle, and each in turn, using just a word or two or a phrase, names something significant about the first decade of her life, birth to ten years. (We emphasize "just a word or two or a phrase" since it's very easy to get warmed up to sharing and run short of time!)

When the circle is completed, those women who have reached the next decade or beyond take one step forward, creating the next circle, and the process is repeated. This continues until the last decade represented in the group is completed. Anyone may pass her turn at any time. For some it may well be that to say "I survived" is enough.

birth ~ 10 years
10 ~ 20
20 ~ 30
30 ~ 40
40 ~ 50
50 ~ 60
60 ~ 70
70 ~ 80

When the circles are completed, ask those who wish to be celebrated as new crones to move to the center, along with the old crones. Others return to the outer circle and sit.

HONORING THE NEW CRONES

The old crones share what it is like for them to be the age they are. Then the new crones talk about their insights, feelings and what they are looking forward to.

The stoles are presented to the new crones with these words:
"As a symbol of your new status, we present you with this stole, weaving together the strands of your life."

The crystals are presented with these words:
"We want you to know that this community supports you in your journey forward, that we praise and bless you, and that we know that we will learn from you. We give you an amethyst crystal to help you in your ongoing transformation."

Any other verbal or physical gifts offered by others may also be given at this time.

CHANT
The crones, new and old, lead the group in a spiral dance, chanting "The Old Women Keep the Beat!" **

SINGING

OPENING THE CIRCLE

FEASTING

VARIATIONS as time permits

Slides/pictures of the new crones, showing the stages of their lives
Discussion of the aging process, acceptance and celebration
Crone meditation

Crone meditation
Relax, etc. . . .

Come, I am going to lead you on a journey. . . . You are walking through a forest of enormous trees. The ground beneath your feet is spongy. The sun is filtering through the trees. It is warm. The smell is sweet and pungent.

53

You come to a large tree with a hole in it. You look in and see a ladder going down. You climb down, unafraid but curious. At the bottom there is a door with a bright brass knob. You turn the knob and the door opens onto a lovely landscape... warm... sunny... with birds, flowers, trees.

You walk along a path that takes you toward water. Sitting on a rock at the edge of the water is a crone ~ a wise older woman. She looks very familiar. She is about your size. Her position as she sits there is one that you frequently take.

You approach her, and as she turns to look at you, you realise you are looking at yourself.

She rises, opens her arms to greet you.

How do you describe this woman? What words would you use? What colors? What music does she make you think of?

(pause 15 seconds)

You move toward her... embrace her... together you begin to walk. She tells you what is most important in her life... what she likes to do... where she lives.

You continue on your journey with your friend. You walk to a meadow where there are birds and flowers. She stoops and picks a flower and gives it to you. She directs you to ask the flower what special gift you shall have as a crone.

You walk further, into a forest, and you meet an animal. Your friend speaks to the animal. You touch and speak to the animal and ask "What is the special gift I will have when I am a crone?"

(pause 30 seconds)

54

When it is time for you to make your return journey, you notice a large bird resting on an outcropping of rock. Your friend calls to the bird. The bird turns toward you, spreads its wings and waits for you to climb on. You say goodbye to your friend the crone and fly up with the bird.

Circling the lovely land . . . and out into a rainbow . . . you finally come back to the place in the beautiful landscape where you found the door. You pause a moment and then open the door . . . climb up the ladder . . . and walk out of the forest . . . back to this circle . . . .

And when you are ready, slowly open your eyes.

* The stole is made of four different-colored 5/8" ribbons, round-braided into a tube about 48" long. The colors may represent whatever you want them to: North, South, East and West; the physical, intellectual, emotional and spiritual aspects of our lives; earth, air, fire and water; favorite colors. Sometimes, woven into the center is a thin black ribbon or thread called the "Cord of Remembering," which honors all women who have gone before us and reminds us of our mortality.

** "The Old Women Keep the Beat" is a background chant on "Keep Simple Ceremonies," words and music by Susan Savell, from The Power of My Love For You; Heartlight Music, Portland, ME, 1986

GRIEF, RAGE AND CELEBRATION

Jane Cunningham, a member of Community, died after a nine-month struggle with cancer. Jane gave to the Community the design for our logo - a circle of women holding hands and singing as we gather our energies and bring our visions into reality.

Community women were with Jane throughout this period, and after her death her husband, Bill, asked us to create and lead the funeral service.

In designing the ritual, we sought to respect the plurality of traditions and expectations represented, to share grief and outrage and to offer comfort.

For instance, we chose the metaphor of the ocean to bridge traditions and to honor Jane's love of the sea. We also invited many people to share the leadership of the service.

This ritual is more personal than any other in this book to honor the woman for whom it was created and those whose grief, rage and celebration we shared.

CASTING THE CIRCLE

INVOCATION

We have come here today to celebrate Jane and her life, to share our memories and her gifts, to mourn her death, to say good-bye and to begin to live again, with her presence very powerfully among us.

LET US PRAY:

GOD OF A THOUSAND NAMES AND FACES, WE COME TO YOU TODAY AS CHILDREN TO THEIR PARENTS AND AS LOVERS TO ONE ANOTHER. WE COME WITH BROKEN HEARTS, AND WE NEED TO BE HELD, TO BE COMFORTED AND SUSTAINED IN OUR GRIEF.

WE COME TO YOU AS WE COME TO THE OCEAN THAT JANE SO DEARLY LOVED - THE OCEAN THAT COVERS US WITH LOVE AND TENDERNESS, HEALING US WITH COOL, CLEAR WATER, HOLDING US AFLOAT, AND INVITING US TO REJOICE IN THE SHEER BEAUTY AND POWER OF OUR INDIVIDUAL AND COMMON LIFE TOGETHER.

HELP US TO ACCEPT THE WAVES OF LOVE AND CARING THAT COME TO US THROUGH ONE ANOTHER, TO CELEBRATE IN OUR GRIEF THE JOY THAT IS JANE, AND TO GROW FROM WHAT SHE HAS GIVEN US AND FROM WHAT SHE HAS CALLED FORTH FROM US.

SONG

"AMAZING GRACE" - EVERYONE SINGS (WE USED A NON-TRADITIONAL VERSION)

STORYTELLING

ONE PERSON RELATES THE STORY OF JANE'S LIFE, THE GIFTS SHE GAVE TO US - BOTH TANGIBLE AND INTANGIBLE - AND THE CHALLENGES SHE LEFT WITH US.

THOSE PRESENT ARE THEN INVITED TO SHARE INDIVIDUAL STORIES OF JANE AND HOW THEIR LIVES WERE ENRICHED BY HER PRESENCE.

"A Song for Jane" *

I SAW YOU FLY
FLY INTO THE OPEN ARMS OF LOVE
I SAW YOU FLY
FLY INTO THE HEART OF EVERYTHING YOU'VE LOVED
YOU LIVE IN ME.

I SAW YOU FLY
FLY INTO THE OPEN ARMS OF LOVE
I SAW YOU FLY
FLY INTO THE HEART OF EVERYTHING YOU'VE LOVED
COME FLY IN ME
I'LL LET YOU BE
THE BEAUTY THAT YOU SAW IN EVERY PART OF ME.

FOR THE CHILDREN

THESE WORDS ARE WRITTEN ESPECIALLY FOR BEN AND SARAH AND MATT AND GABRIEL, FOR ALL THE CHILDREN WHO KNEW AND LOVED JANE, AND FOR THE CHILD IN EACH OF US ADULTS WHO LOVED TO PLAY AND SING AND DANCE AND LAUGH AND CRY WITH HER.

IT IS ONE OF THE GREAT MIRACLES OF LIFE THAT EACH ONE OF US IS SO UNIQUE, SO SPECIAL, THAT WE LEAVE A HOLE IN THE WORLD WHEN WE DIE. A HOLE IN THE HEARTS OF THOSE WE HAVE LOVED. WE ALSO LEAVE A SENSE OF CELEBRATION ... THE FEELING THAT THE LIVES OF OTHER PEOPLE ARE RICHER AND FULLER AND MORE COLORFUL FOR HAVING KNOWN AND LOVED US. BOTH OF THESE FEELINGS ARE TRUE AND GO TOGETHER. WHAT THEY HAVE IN COMMON IS A PROFOUND SENSE OF THE UNIQUENESS OF EACH PERSON.

AND SO IT IS WITH JANE. JANE WAS DIFFERENT FROM ANYONE ELSE IN THE WHOLE WORLD. THERE NEVER WAS ANYONE JUST LIKE HER, AND THERE NEVER WILL BE AGAIN. WHAT A REMARKABLE IDEA THAT IS! IF

WE WERE ALL THE SAME, IT WOULDN'T MATTER SO MUCH WHEN ONE PERSON DIED. THE LOSS OF SOMEONE WE LOVE IS SO PAINFUL AND HURTS SO MUCH BECAUSE OF THAT UNIQUENESS. WE CAN AND WE WILL FIND OTHER PEOPLE TO LOVE, BUT EACH LOVE — LIKE OUR LOVE FOR JANE — IS SPECIAL AND DIFFERENT FROM ALL OTHERS.

WHEN SOMETHING HAPPENS TO MAKE US VERY SAD, SOMETHING LIKE THE DEATH OF A WONDERFUL, BELOVED PERSON LIKE JANE, WE LEARN SOMETHING NEW AND IMPORTANT ABOUT HOW WONDERFUL IT IS TO BE ALIVE. THE HEARTBREAK OF HAVING A PERSON WE LOVE DIE TEACHES US JUST HOW VALUABLE EACH PERSON IS — JUST HOW PRECIOUS AND SPECIAL. SUCH AN EXPERIENCE TEACHES US THAT LIFE IS SACRED.

ALTHOUGH IT FEELS AS IF JANE IS TOTALLY GONE, WE COME TO LEARN THAT NOBODY EVER DIES COMPLETELY. WHEN SOMEONE DIES, WE DISCOVER HOW MUCH SHE HAS LEFT BEHIND. EACH PERSON WHO LIVES CHANGES THE WORLD IN SOME LARGE OR SMALL WAY AND LEAVES MUCH OF HERSELF TO THOSE WHO LIVE AFTERWARD. CHILDREN, OF COURSE, ARE A BEAUTIFUL GIFT TO LEAVE THE WORLD. JANE LOVED EACH OF YOU DEARLY AND SHE DEEPLY BELIEVED THAT EACH ONE OF YOU IS SUCH A BEAUTIFUL GIFT TO THE WORLD.

A TEACHER MAY LEAVE BEHIND LOTS OF CHILDREN WHO WILL REMEMBER THAT SHE COULD TEACH IN SUCH A WAY THAT EVERY CHILD HAD FUN AND DIDN'T EVER FEEL DUMB. A HOUSE PAINTER MAY LEAVE BEHIND A LOT OF HAPPY FAMILIES LIVING IN PRETTY HOUSES. A GOOD COOK LEAVES BEHIND LOTS OF WONDERFUL RECIPES FOR PEOPLE TO ENJOY FOR GENERATIONS. A MOTHER TEACHES HER BABY SPECIAL LULLABIES THAT HER MOTHER TAUGHT HER AND THAT HER CHILDREN WILL TEACH THEIR CHILDREN. A FIREFIGHTER SAVES THE LIFE OF A CHILD WHO BECOMES A DOCTOR AND SAVES OTHER PEOPLE'S LIVES.

JANE LEAVES BEHIND MANY SPECIAL MEMORIES AND DEEDS WHICH WILL LIVE IN OUR HEARTS FOR WEEKS AND MONTHS AND YEARS AND YEARS TO COME. THEY WILL BE A PART OF ALL OF US FOR ALL OF OUR LIVES.

AND THERE IS ONE THING I KNOW JANE WOULD WANT US TO REMEMBER ABOUT LIVING THE LIVES THAT HAVE BEEN GIVEN TO US: TO LIVE AND LOVE AND LAUGH AND CRY AND <u>BE REAL</u> IN EVERY MOMENT. TO GIVE YOUR OWN VERY BEST, SPECIAL SELF TO THE PEOPLE AROUND YOU. JUST AS SHE DID WITH US. THAT IS THE VERY BEST KIND OF GOODBYE THAT WE CAN GIVE TO JANE!

WORDS OF HEALING AND RENEWAL

THE WATERS COME — RISING, SWIRLING, POUNDING WATERS OF LIFE AND DEATH. WE FIGHT THEM, WE ARE TOSSED ABOUT BY THEM, WE ARE EXHAUSTED BY THEM — WE ARE CLEANSED BY THEM. LIKE THE OCEAN, GOD'S LOVE, THE LOVE AT THE HEART OF THE UNIVERSE, IS A MYSTERY, UNFATHOMABLE IN ITS DEPTH. BUT WE KNOW THAT THE STORM PASSES, THE FLOODS RECEDE, AND THE BLUE-GREEN WATER REMAINS.

THE OCEAN OF THAT LOVE CONTINUES TO COVER US WITH GENEROSITY AND WITH FORGIVENESS FOR WHAT WE HAVE LEFT UNDONE WITH JANE. THE OCEAN OF THAT LOVE NOW HOLDS JANE AND US IN NEW AND TRANSFORMED WAYS. AS WE OPEN OURSELVES TO THAT PRESENCE, WE CAN BEGIN TO LIVE, TO ENJOY LIFE MORE PROFOUNDLY, MORE CLEARLY THAN EVER BEFORE.

SONG

" SONG OF THE SOUL" ** (EVERYONE SINGS)

BENEDICTION

"BLESSINGS OF GOD BE UPON YOU" ***

MAY THE BLESSINGS OF GOD BE UPON YOU
MAY GOD'S PEACE ABIDE WITH YOU
MAY GOD'S PRESENCE ILLUMINATE YOUR HEART
NOW AND FOREVER MORE.

SINGING

OPENING THE CIRCLE

* WORDS AND MUSIC BY SUSAN SAVELL ON THE AUDIO
CASSETTE THE POWER OF MY LOVE FOR YOU , HEART LIGHT MUSIC,
BIDDEFORD POOL , MAINE , 1986.

** WORDS AND MUSIC BY CRIS WILLIAMSON ON THE AUDIO
CASSETTE THE CHANGER AND THE CHANGED , BIRD ANKLES MUSIC,
1975, OLIVIA RECORDS .

*** FROM THE SUFI TRADITION , A VERSION OF THIS SONG IS ON THE
AUDIO CASSETTE RITUAL SONGS BY THE COLORADO MIDWIVES
ASSOCIATION , SILVER WAVE RECORDS , PO BOX 7943 , BOULDER,
COLORADO 80306, 1983.

Seasons
of the
Earth

The Sigils *

 Imbolc:~a five-branched stave, representing the upraised hand with spread fingers.

 Alban Eilir, Ostara:~the vernal equinox: a circle with two sprouting horns, signifying the seed putting forth its shoots.

 Beltane:~The Tree of Life with six side branches~the Maypole and maybushes.

 Alban Hefin:~the summer solstice: an open curve signifying the open leaves of the fully developed plant.

 Lammas, Lughnassad:~a semicircle bisected by a line, signifying the stalk of wheat and a loaf of bread baked from that grain.

 Mabon, Alban Elfed:~the autumnal equinox: a stylized dying plant.

 Samhain:~a knot of protection

 Yule:~the winter solstice, Alban Arthuan: an enclosure containing dots representing either the seed in the ground or people sheltering from wintry weather.

* from The Pagan Book of Days by Nigel Pennick, Destiny Books, Rochester, VT 1992

64

IMBOLC

IMBOLC IS THE FIRST OF THE CROSS-QUARTER DAYS, OCCURING ON FEBRUARY 1, AND CELEBRATES THE APPROACHING END OF WINTER. THIS CELEBRATION FREQUENTLY FOCUSES ON THE RETURN OF THE LIGHT AFTER THE DARKNESS OF WINTER. AS A VARIATION, THIS RITUAL WILL BEGIN TO DEVELOP THE THEME OF THE CYCLE OF GROWTH THAT CARRIES THROUGH THE OTHER CROSS-QUARTER DAYS.

BRIGIT MCCALLUM FIRST SHARED THIS RITUAL WITH FSC IN FEBRUARY OF 1991.

MATERIALS

CLEAR PLASTIC 5 OUNCE DISPOSABLE CUPS, ONE FOR EACH
   PARTICIPANT, FILLED 2/3 FULL WITH POTTING SOIL
BEAN SEEDS, ENOUGH SO THAT EACH PARTICIPANT MAY HAVE
   3 OR SO
PITCHER OF WATER
SMALL PAPER OR PLASTIC BAGS

CASTING THE CIRCLE

INTRODUCING THE RITUAL

THIS IS IMBOLC, THE ANCIENT FESTIVAL MARKING THE APPROACHING END OF WINTER AND CELEBRATING THE FIRST STIRRINGS OF THE NEW SEED IN THE COLD, DARK SOIL. THE THREEFOLD GODDESS IS TRANSFORMED FROM HER ASPECT OF THE CRONE OF WINTER INTO THE MAIDEN OF SPRING, THE BRIDE WHO WILL SOON BE PREGNANT WITH NEW LIFE.*

THROUGHOUT THE PAST WINTER, WE HAVE BEEN DEEP WITHIN OURSELVES, SHELTERING FROM THE COLD. WE HAVE BEEN

65

DEEP WITHIN THE EARTH, RESTING AND BEING RENEWED, NURTURED BY THE DARKNESS. IT IS TIME NOW TO AWAKEN FROM SLEEP, TO FEEL THE SEEDS OF NEW LIFE BEGINNING TO MOVE WITHIN US.

WE ARE ALL FACED WITH NEW CHALLENGES. SOME ARE CLEARLY VISIBLE ON THE HORIZON; OTHERS ARE STILL HIDDEN. WE MAY NOT KNOW HOW WE WILL RESPOND. TO MEET TOMORROW'S CHALLENGES, WE WILL HAVE TO BE WHO WE HAVE NEVER BEEN. THE POTENTIAL IS THERE, GROWING IN THE DARKNESS OF POSSIBILITY, OUT FROM THE MYSTERY. THERE IS A TIME FOR MANIFESTATION, FOR SHOWING ALL OUR POWER AND STRENGTH, BUT THAT TIME IS NOT YET. NOW IS THE TIME FOR THE SILENCE, THE WAITING, KNOWING THAT DEEP WORK IS GOING ON.

IMBOLC IS THE TIME OF THE FIRST MOVEMENT OF THE SEED WHICH HAS LAIN SO STILL IN THE DEPTHS. ITS FIRST MOVE IS NOT UPWARD, HOWEVER, BUT DOWN. THE MOVEMENT INTO ROOTING WILL SUPPORT AND NURTURE THE LATER GROWTH TOWARD THE SUN. FIRST, THE SEED MUST ESTABLISH ITSELF IN THE EARTH, TO BECOME ABLE TO DRAW IN NUTRIENTS. IN ORDER TO BE STRONG OUT IN THE WORLD, WE TAKE THE TIME TO PUT DOWN ROOTS INTO THAT WHICH SUSTAINS US, EVEN THOUGH WE MAY NOT KNOW HOW TO NAME IT. WE PUT ROOTS DOWN INTO THE MYSTERY AND LEARN WHO AND WHAT IS THERE TO FEED US.

WE WILL GO WITHIN, TO THE PLACE WHERE THE NEW SEED LIES. WE GO DEEPLY, TO SEE AND LISTEN AND LEARN. WE GO THERE TO CONNECT AND COMMIT TO THE NEW LIFE WHICH BEGINS TO MOVE WITHIN US.

MEDITATION

RELAX, ETC. . . . .

LET US JOURNEY INWARD NOW, AWAY FROM THE NEWS OF THE OUTER WORLD, AWAY FROM THE WORRIES AND STRUGGLES OF THE DAY, TO THAT WHICH IS NOT YET. LET US JOURNEY WITHIN TO WHERE THE NEW SEED IS PLANTED.

BE AWARE OF YOUR BREATHING NOW, FEEL THE PULSE
OF LIFE IN YOU . . . LET IT BE STILL. GO TO THAT PLACE
DEEP INSIDE YOU . . . THAT DARK PLACE OF ABSOLUTE
STILLNESS . . .

LET YOURSELF ROAM NOW, OVER INNER LANDSCAPES,
TO THE SITE WHERE THIS NEW SEED IS GROWING, THE SEED
WHICH WILL YIELD ITS MYSTERY AND POWER IN THE MONTHS
TO COME. WHERE DO YOU FIND IT? WHAT ARE THE
CONDITIONS THERE? IS IT WARM . . . COLD . . . ARE THERE
ANY SMELLS . . . ? DO YOU SEE ANY COLORS . . . ? HOW DOES
IT FEEL . . . ?

LET YOUR EYES SEE AS DEEPLY AS YOU NEED TO IN
ORDER TO SEE THIS SEED AS IT IS GROWING. WHAT DOES
IT LOOK LIKE? IS IT SMALL . . . ? LARGE . . . ? DEEP . . . ?
SHALLOW . . . ? WHAT IS THE SOIL LIKE . . . ? IS THERE
ANYTHING ELSE THERE . . . ? HOW DOES THIS PLACE FEEL . . . ?

WATCH NOW. THE SEED STIRS. A TINY CRACK APPEARS,
AND THEN, SLOWLY, SO SLOWLY, THE CRACK GROWS AND THE FIRST
MOVEMENT HAPPENS, BUT IT IS NOT UPWARDS TOWARD THE
LIGHT, BUT DOWN. A SLENDER, FRAGILE, YET INCREDIBLY
STRONG ROOT BEGINS TO EMERGE. THE ROOT MUST BE FIRMLY
SET BEFORE THE UPWARD GROWTH CAN BEGIN. THIS TAPROOT
WILL BRING IN WATER AND NUTRIENTS TO THE BURSTING
SEED, ANCHORING IT AND DRAWING IN ALL IT NEEDS.

LOOK AT THE SOIL THIS ROOT MUST PASS THROUGH.
ARE THERE OBSTACLES PREVENTING IT FROM GOING VERY DEEP . . . ?
WHAT WILL IT NEED IN ORDER TO ANCHOR WELL AND DEEPLY . . . ?
LET YOURSELF CREATE THE CONDITIONS FOR ITS PROGRESS.
ALLOW THIS TO HAPPEN IN ANY MAGICAL WAY THAT IS NEEDED.

(PAUSE 1 MINUTE)

WHAT IS GROWING IN YOU . . . ? DO YOU RECOGNIZE
IT, OR IS IT STILL HIDDEN IN THE MYSTERY . . . ? WHAT NEW
FORM IS THE LIFE FORCE GATHERING TO BE BIRTHED IN THE

67

MONTHS TO COME ...? WHAT NEW EXPRESSION OF LIFE'S LOVE FOR ITSELF WILL COME IN AND THROUGH YOU ...? WHAT DO YOU NEED TO NURTURE THIS GROWTH ...? WHAT DO YOU NEED TO HONOR AND RESPECT IT ...? WHAT IS THE SOIL LIKE IN YOUR LIFE AT THIS TIME ...? WHERE IS IT THAT YOU ARE ROOTED ...? WHAT FEEDS YOU ...? ARE THERE OTHER ROOTS SHARING THIS SOIL ...? IS ANYTHING INTERFERING WITH YOUR CAPACITY TO NURTURE YOUR GROWTH ...? WHAT MAY HAVE TO WAIT UNTIL THE NEW GROWTH IS FURTHER ALONG?

(PAUSE 1 MINUTE)

LEAVE THIS SEED NOW, WITH THIS NEW ROOT ... LET IT CONTINUE TO GROW. AS YOU RETURN UP THROUGH THE LAYERS OF SOIL, BRING WITH YOU THE KNOWLEDGE THAT YOU ARE BEING STRENGTHENED AND TRANSFORMED, BEING MADE READY TO MEET WHATEVER NEW CHALLENGE IS WAITING FOR YOU.

IN THIS TIME OF VIOLENCE, OF FEAR, OF OPPRESSION IT IS HARD TO BRING NEW LIFE INTO BEING, YET THAT IS JUST WHAT THE WEB OF LIFE REQUIRES. THERE ARE RENTS IN THE WEB FROM THE FORCES OF VIOLENCE AND OPPRESSION. EACH OF US IS NEEDED, SO WE MUST STAY CONNECTED AND BIRTH WHAT WE CAN. AND WE REMEMBER THE OLD TRADITIONS, THE CELEBRATIONS OF FIRE AND LOVE.

TAKE A DEEP BREATH NOW. BEGIN TO FEEL THE AIR AROUND YOU ... THE FLOOR SUPPORTING YOU. SLOWLY COME BACK TO THIS ROOM WHERE WE WAIT FOR NEW GROWTH ... WHERE WE SING AND WE DANCE AS WE WAIT, FOR IT IS A FINE THING, INDEED, FOR WOMEN TO BIRTH, IN ALL THE MYRIAD WAYS THAT WE DO.

PLANTING THE SEED

DIVIDE INTO GROUPS OF FOUR TO DISCUSS ANY INSIGHTS AND TO PLANT YOUR SEEDS. YOU MIGHT

LIKE TO SHARE WHAT NEW GROWTH, REPRESENTED BY THESE SEEDS, IS COMING INTO YOUR LIFE.

THE CLEAR PLASTIC CUPS WILL ALLOW YOU, IN THE NEXT DAYS, TO WATCH THE GROWTH OF YOUR TAPROOT.

SONG: "MY ROOTS GO DOWN" **

SINGING

OPENING THE CIRCLE

* PENNICK, NIGEL, _THE PAGAN BOOK OF DAYS: A GUIDE TO THE FESTIVALS, TRADITIONS, AND SACRED DAYS OF THE YEAR_, (ROCHESTER, VT: DESTINY BOOKS, 1992), p. 14.

** WORDS AND MUSIC BY SARAH PIRTLE, RECORDED ON THE AUDIO CASSETTE _TWO HANDS HOLD THE EARTH_. TO ORDER, CONTACT "A GENTLE WIND" AT DISCOVERY CENTER, 65 MAIN ST., SHELBURNE FALLS, MA 01390.

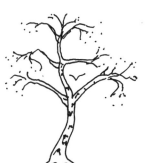

BELTANE

    The festival of Beltane takes place on May 1 and begins at sunset of the preceding day.

    The majority of this ritual was originally done by Brigit McCallum shortly after fourteen women engineering students were killed in Montreal, December 6, 1989.

    As preparation for the ritual, those who will participate are invited to burn and extinguish, the evening before the ritual, a candle or lantern and bring it to the ritual. It will represent their home fires.

MATERIALS

        Beltane altar cloth*
        Extra candles for those who may not have brought their own
        Cauldron and sterno for Beltane fire
        Flowers and brightly colored ribbons to decorate the altar and
                ritual space

PURIFYING

    Participants are invited to be smudged with sage or some other purifying herbs as they enter the ritual space.

CASTING THE CIRCLE

    As each woman names herself, she is invited to "bring" her home fire and place it before her in the circle.

INTRODUCING THE RITUAL

Beltane is a festival of great celebration, honoring fertility, growth and passion. It calls upon all deities whose realms involve growth and fertility. Spring planting has been completed, crops are growing, and we are now joyfully moving into the summer season. Fire is central to the Beltane celebration, representing the mystical center of life.

As we prepare for this celebration, we are aware that, with the advent of patriarchal society, the sacred fires of the goddess were stolen and became remembered as the sole province of male passion. The perception and use of fire changed from that of a healing, creative force to one of a tool for destruction and violence, associated particularly with war. Through violence that continues today, the power of woman was nearly obliterated.

But this is a turning time — we dare to remember the abuse, the pain, our own experience of violation, and to connect it to that of others, past and present. It is a time of re-turning to our power and of remembering that power to be within. The sacredness of woman returns to life in this time of spring as we feel the fire of the goddess within us. In ways great and small, we bring this fire into all we do. We will not forget again.

MEDITATION**

Relax, etc.

As we move together into this meditation, we will draw in and work with earth-fire. Know that it is your intention which guides the work you will do; it is your intention which will focus the fire. If at any time you do not wish to proceed with the meditation as guided, create the intention you need in order to bring in images that will be helpful and healing for you. You have choice at all times in this work.

Take a deep breath and slowly release it.

Now see or feel roots coming from you and going down into the earth. Let them go down — healthy, strong, full of life. Roots moving down and down... down through the layers of the earth. See or feel them going through sand... through rock... through water... through the bones of our ancestors... all the way until they reach the center of the earth. To the fiery core of the earth we walk upon. Yours are roots that have the capacity to carry the fire, becoming bearers and carriers of fire. As they reach into the fire, let them begin to draw it up.... Draw the fire up through your roots, letting it move through every tendril and fibre of root, returning toward the surface, coming back through the earth and into you.... Let that fire, the fire of the earth, come into you. You can contain this fire. Feel its warmth, its life within you.

(Pause 1 minute)

Let the fire grow now, let it expand until it fills all of you.

(Pause 15 seconds)

Breathing in and out, you are full of this fire. Strong fire of the earth. Let the fire continue to grow now, joining us together so that we form a ring of fire. We are a circle of fire — strong, healthy, healing fire. Let this fire grow now until it fills the room... filling the room with fire. Let the fire energy continue to grow now, focused by your healing intention, this fire that is a cleansing fire, an energizing and creating fire. Imagine it touching all who need healing, filling all places of violence with its transforming flames.

(Pause 1 minute)

Bring the fire back into the room now. Bring it back into the circle ... back into you. Let it find its resting place in you now.... Know that you can make it as large, wide, or tall — or as concentrated and laser-pointed — as you need, to do the work that is needed.

Let it become an ember now, a live, burning ember, burning within you. The same fire that burns at the core of the earth burns in you. This is the spirit of life in you — without it you are not whole, you deny your power. This is the sacred flame in you.

Search within your body now, and find a place to keep this ember. Place it carefully, knowing that it will be safe and available to you anytime you wish to use it.

(Pause 1 minute)

Slowly now, come back to this room and to this circle of women. Feel the floor supporting you, and be aware of the ember you carry inside you. When you are ready, slowly and gently open your eyes.

DISCUSSION

As you are moved, in small or large groups, share any insights, feelings and/or visions experienced in the meditation.

THE BELTANE FIRE

If you have been in small groups, return to stand in one large circle. Someone says:

"Traditionally, home fires were extinguished on the eve of the Beltane holiday, to be relit the following day from the community's central hearth, which represented the divine spark of life carried by each of us. We now look to the dark fire of our altar/hearth and remember the violations experienced by women, past and present."

Invite the participants to call out memories of abuses experienced by women, specific or general (e.g. the Burning Times, the fourteen women killed in Montreal, etc.)

73

Someone says, as she lights the Beltane (sterno) fire on the altar/ hearth:

"We now call the fire of the goddess to life and, in so doing, call forth her power for the world. As we each light our own fires from this community hearth, we reclaim the power of women. The fire of life lives within us, and with the constant renewal and support of this community, we take it out into the world."

Each woman in her turn brings her candle to the altar and lights it from the Beltane fire in the cauldron. These will remain lit as all leave the ritual space at the end of the ritual.

CONE OF POWER***

As the individual fires are being lit, the group sings "Many-Eyed Woman."**** When all have returned to the circle, gradually increase the volume and tempo of the song to build a cone of power. After the energy peaks and releases, be sure to ground it before opening the circle.

SINGING

OPENING THE CIRCLE

The home-fire candles are not extinguished at the end of the ritual. With them, each woman carries the fire of the goddess from the community hearth to her own home.

* The Beltane altar cloth may be designed to simulate the preparation of the earth on the site of the Beltane fire. A grid of four parallel horizontal lines is crossed by four vertical lines, creating nine squares. The fire is laid in the center square. See Pennick, op. cit. p. 16

74

**The meditation is an adaptation of one done by Lyri Merrill of Sanchin School of Self Defense for Women, Jamaica Plain, MA. Used with permission.

***See the Unbinding Ritual, p. 126.

****"Many-Eyed Woman," words and music by Brigit McCallum, is sung as follows:

MANY EYED WO-MAN I SEE THROUGH THE RAIN ~ I

See THROUGH THE SHA ~ DOWS AND I SEE THROUGH THE PAIN ~ I

See THROUGH THE FI ~ RES AND I RISE ONCE A~GAIN ~ yes I

ri ~ SE ~ ENCE A~GAIN!

LAMMAS

Lammas is the cross-quarter day representing the fullness of growth, just before harvest, celebrated on August first.

Materials

Fruit
Flowers
Acorns
Brown candle
Amulet materials
  Thin red ribbon in one-yard lengths, one for each person
  Self-hardening red clay, enough for each person to make a small disc of approximately two inches
  Pointed manicure sticks (orange sticks) or other pointed tool to carve design in clay and to make a hole in the clay

CASTING THE CIRCLE

In addition to the usual candles, light a brown candle for the ripening of the earth, for the fullness of bearing. Each woman, when naming herself in the circle, invokes a fruit, grain, seed or fruit-bearing tree.

(Pause 1 minute)

This is Lammas — the time of reaping what was conceived in winter and sown in spring. As Nature shares fruit, grain, vegetable, seed and flower, so we receive the fulfillment of the promises made to ourselves in mid-winter.

Notice the fruit that ripens on the branches and vines of your life.

(Pause 1-2 minutes)

See what you planted with hope and intention, and nurtured with your prayer and understanding.... See, amid the lovely scents, shapes and colors, how what you protected, nurtured and fertilized comes now to fulfillment.

(Pause 2 minutes)

What grows in your field, orchard or garden?

(Pause)

Let that which is full and complete be harvested with your acceptance, gratitude and celebration! Know that this will nurture and sustain you now and through the dark resting time, when you dream and prepare for the growth of the next cycle, and make new promises to yourself.

You save some of the seeds for planting in the spring, for future harvests.

77

INTRODUCING THE RITUAL

Lammas is a time when we witness the ripening of what was sown earlier, and acknowledge the completion of a cycle. Some of what we harvest is for use now, most is stored for sustenance through the leaner times. We also remember to save some of our harvest for planting in a new cycle — a cycle which may begin right away or after incubation through the winter.

In the ancient Lammas festivals of central and northern Europe, the sign of this celebration was a semicircle bisected by a line,* representing the harvested grain and the loaf of bread made from that grain. The traditional color of the autumn season was brown.

MEDITATION

Relax, etc.
As you sit or lie supported by the floor, your attention goes to a sweet and sacred place, a place of quiet, peace and reflection, where there is sky and green, shade and sun, wind and water.

(Pause)

You drink in the sensations of this place and this moment with your skin, your eyes, your ears and your nose. With every cell, you experience this fullness of being.

78

What seeds will you keep for the bearing out in future growth challenges?

(Pause 1 minute)

Now, you gently return from your reflection to the sweet and sacred place where you have rested, again drinking in, through all your senses, the gifts of this season in your life. You place your handful of seeds in your pocket.

(Pause)

Your attention is drawn gently back to this land, this building, where you lie or sit, supported by the floor, among these women. When you are ready, slowly open your eyes.

DISCUSSION

Break into small groups. Each woman takes a piece of fruit and has an opportunity to talk about what is coming to completion for her. As you talk, each woman also takes a piece of clay and makes a small amulet, placing a hole in the top for the red ribbon. Carve the sign of Lammas on the amulet.**

Return to one large circle.

Each woman is invited to move to the center of the circle to take an acorn and talk about the future growth she anticipates for the spring.

79

SINGING

OPENING THE CIRCLE

* op. cit. Pennick, p.17.

** Allow the amulets to dry fully before being worn, to prevent breaking. They can be decorated later to each person's taste.

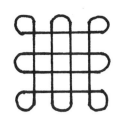

SAMHAIN

Samhain (pronounced sah-wane) marks the end of the Celtic year. Celebration begins on the evening of October 31 and continues into the next day. Samhain is a time of reflection - of looking back on the year — and a time to begin settling in for the winter.

MATERIALS

Cauldron
Samhain candle
New Year candle
Paper*, pens, crayons to make effigies
Drums and rattles

CASTING THE CIRCLE

In addition to the usual candles, light the Samhain candle. Someone says:

"As this year comes to an end, I light this candle for the burning away of that which is no longer needed in our lives, for the clearing of the harvested field to make way for the growth of spring."

INTRODUCING THE RITUAL

This is Samhain. Our harvest is in, stored for use through the coming months of darkness. The results of our work and actions through the year have been manifested. There have been many celebrations, sadnesses and victories this year.

In this ritual, we will walk back through the thoughts and actions, the colors and feelings of these past months to find any ills, any disappointments, any losses that remain at this time of completion. As we walk, images may form of things we wish to clear away, things we don't need to carry into the new year. Some hurts may not be ready for release, but we may be able to lessen their hold on our lives.

After our walk, we will create, in silence, an effigy (see glossary) of whatever image has come to us that we wish to clear away.

SPIRAL WALK

In preparation for the walk, teach one of the following chants, to be sung as you walk.

We suggest the chant "Baba La Gum Bala,** a Swahili harvest chant. Alternatively, you could use "Snake Woman Shedding Her Skin"**

Sing slowly, repeat until all seem familiar with it.

Moving Meditation:***

Stand in a circle, begin to chant quietly. Someone says:

"As we chant and circle our energies, we will walk back through this past year of growth to examine what can be cast off to clear the land in preparation for the plantings of spring. Let the thinking, rational part of you be at rest; let yourself be open to feeling any sadnesses, losses and disappointments that have been a part of your year.

As you walk, you will find that the spirits who guide you in life, the spirits of your ancestors and the spirits of your descendents are all available to help you. Call on them for wisdom and insight as you walk."

One person leads the group, _very slowly,_ into a loose spiral and out again, with the chant continuing for about 15 minutes.

The spiral leader then returns the group to a large circle to finish the chant.

CREATING EFFIGIES

With the circle keeping the silence after the chanting has finished, someone says:

"Now take paper and make a representation of your hurt, your sadness, your disappointment — make it manifest in preparation for burning it to clear your field for its rest. As you work, again feel the emotion, the loss, the disappointment of what was not done, what was done too strongly, what was attempted that failed, what was hoped for that did not grow."

BURNING EFFIGIES

When all are ready, each woman who wants to talks briefly about her effigy, then sets fire to it from the Samhain candle. She drops the effigy into the cauldron, saying "I clear my field of this _____." The rest of the circle calls support with drums, rattles, and voices.

GROUNDING

Conclude with all in a circle. Take several deep breaths in and out, eyes closed, hands touching.

Light a candle for the new year, inviting in the changes that will come. Someone says:

"The increasing darkness of this season begins to pull at us to turn inward — to go in and down into the resting time. In clearing away, we allow the turning inward to envelop us.

Feel the pull into the darkness, the resting time of winter."

End on this quiet note.

SINGING

OPENING THE CIRCLE

*   Should be very lightweight, easily-burned paper to avoid smoke production.

**   "Baba La Gum Bala" is on the audio cassette <u>Pilgrim Warrior: Songs and Chants Celebrating Women's Spirituality and Politics</u>, 15 Abbott st., Greenfield, MA. 01301. "Snake Woman," words and music by Starhawk, is on the audio cassette <u>Chants: Ritual Music</u>, produced by the Reclaiming Community, P.O. Box 14404, San Francisco, CA 94114.

***   The lights should be turned down, if possible and if safe, to minimize sensory distraction. Check the area to be walked, moving anything that might be tripped over so that attention can be given to the reflection, not to what's underfoot.

Celebrating the Fool
An April Foola Ritual

Not usually included in traditional or mystical calendars, April Foola has, nevertheless, become a firmly established ritual celebration at Feminist Spiritual Community. A number of women have been involved in creating this ritual over the years, but most years the celebration has been the work (a.k.a. play) of heather alexander, unofficial FSC Jester. We have included a number of "ritual possibilities" here; you may wish to choose those which best fit your group and time line; or, better still, make up your own.

Materials:
    Basket of names for the Renaming circle
    Fairy Dust ☆
    Pinwheel, bubblestuff or squeaky toy
      for casting the circle

Introducing the Ritual
The fool is the part of us that connects unconsciously to the greater universal whole that contains all possibilities. It is the fool who urges the personality away from lethargy toward enlightenment and transformation without fear of the future. Whenever change happens, the fool in us is activated.

When the fool comes, the time is right for your kid to emerge. If you try to hang onto logic or rationality, you are likely to get stuck in a hard place. The fool in you is pure spontaneity, getting in touch with your unacknowledged impulses and unprepared responses to the world. The fool moves from within you. It is not the clear calm voice of the inner sage, but the carefree, irrational impulse — the irrepressible surge of energy that propels you into something. The fool enjoys a charming, playful sense of life, a willingness to experience things.

The universe seems to like those who are open and willing to be moved by their fools; it blesses them with growth and delight. It helps them learn.

Remember: no matter how routine your life seems at the moment, the forces underlying that normalcy are mysterious and unpredictable in the extreme.

Candlelighting

First candle: for all the new women, to give them courage to endure tonight's ordeal, and for them to know that it's not always like this.

Second candle: for those who knew better than to come tonight.

Third candle: for all who foolishly came tonight.

Fourth candle; for our sister community in El Salvador. May they have not only strength and hope, but foolishness as well.

Renaming Circle

In this new age we just aren't "with it" if we go around with names like Mary or Joyce or Dianne. To get into the true spirit of the times we need a "NEW AGE" name. Fate will choose your name for you. In this basket you will find the one that is right for you. NO PEEKING! Reach in and take one, and then we will go around the circle re-naming ourselves.

(You may make up your own names or photo-copy the list at the end of the ritual and cut them apart for the basket.)

Casting the Sacred Foolishness Circle

Circle around with a pinwheel and let each woman blow on it
or
Pass a bottle of bubblestuff and let each woman blow a bubble
or
Use a squeaky toy and circle around squeaking it behind each woman

Invocation of the Four Directions

Spirit of the East, of those airheads who are so spaced out that they don't seem to make contact with earth, especially those we must depend upon to guide us when we face miles of serious government red tape...

Blow the winds which sweep out the cobwebs.

Spirit of the South, of all the truly irascible people we encounter, the ones who bring a lifetime of repressed anger to any small thing that goes wrong, especially the rush hour drivers who honk at us if we happen to be in their way...

Send us the fires of infectious laughter.

Spirit of the West, of all the people who spend hours crying on our shoulders and whom we never see when they are happy, our "foul weather" friends...

Throw us a towel.

Spirit of the North, of the stolid ones who never see humor in anything, those who believe life is to be plodded through and can't stand to see us dance along...

Tickle our funny bones!

We call in all these directions and sprinkle them with a little grain of foolishness. Let's cry out in unison, " LIGHTEN UP!"

(Toss some fairy dust in each direction.)

April Foola's Chakras

Now you may ask me about the chakras.

They are cute little rainbow-colored swirling vortices of energy in various parts of the body.

The FIRST, which is red, is the root chakra. It is the part of the body that makes the whoopie cushion go whoopie when you sit down. If this chakra is feeling just a trifle out of balance, I recommend Preparation H.

The SECOND, which is orange, is a little devil of a swirling vortex. It is the place that gets a little tingle, sometimes at the oddest moments. Sometimes it is more than a _little_ tingle — it could be, shall we say, lustful urges? Or shall we say libidinal surges? It is the home of the little curled up kundalini serpent, and when she is unleashed, I can only say "Watch out!"

The THIRD chakra is yellow. It is the solar plexis, the solar-powered bodhi battery. The big question here is: is yours an innie or an outie?

The green FOURTH chakra, the heart, is what they write all those love songs about, or at least it is what they think they write all those love songs about. I, myself, think that they are writing them about that sneaky curled-up kundalini of a second chakra, but never mind.

The FIFTH chakra is blue and is located at the throat. The throat chakra can sometimes get one into deep trouble, and leads to foot-in-mouth disease when other people cannot bear to hear the truth.

The SIXTH chakra is indigo. It is the brow chakra, and the question here is: high-brow or low-brow? Those with the high-brow chakra are fastidious and fussy, and those with the low-brow can get down and dirty. This is also the home of the third eye. If you are not seeing the world clearly, may I suggest the use of third eye glasses?

The SEVENTH chakra is the glorious crown chakra. It is represented as a thousand petalled lotus with a blue pearl in the center. To keep it bright & well-conditioned, may I suggest the use of Pert?

Last, we have the CLOWN chakra. It is right next to the funny bone and is red-and-white polka-dotted. It is really the most important chakra to have open. It is the one which will teach you the importance of Rule #6, which is: never take yourself too seriously!

April Foola's Chakra Guide

crown chakra (use Pert)

3rd eye or brow chakra

throat chakra (foot in mouth)

heart chakra (unbroken condition)

solar plexis, bodhi battery

the most important chakras - the clown chakras. note that there are 2 of them

that naughty 2nd chakra!

the aura
we'll get into that another time.

root chakra (whoopie!)

Ms. Guided Meditation

This is similar to a "mad-lib" but sillier. In a mad lib, a story is written with key words left out. The words are filled in by going around the room, asking people to supply an adjective, adverb, noun, etc. as called for, to fill in the missing parts of the story. When all blanks are filled, the meditation is read aloud.

We're going on a (adjective) journey, inward, to find your (adjective) guide. Sit (adverb), relax, take a deep (noun). Let all the (plural noun) of the day (verb) (adverb) down through your (body part) into the (noun). Take another (adjective) (noun). Let it out. You are very (verb, past tense).

You find yourself on a (adjective) path that leads into a (adjective) forest. You hear (plural noun) calling to one another as you walk. You think to yourself, this is such a (adjective) place. You (verb) on for (number) minutes until you come to a (adjective) clearing. There, sitting upon a (noun) you see a wise old (noun). "Are you my (adjective) guide?" you ask. "You bet your (body part) the (adjective) (same noun as wise old...) replies. "Am so pleased" you say, "Ive been (verb ending in "ing") for you all my life."

"I have a (adjective) gift for you," the (adjective) one says. "And a message. (Time of day) to bed and (time of day) to rise, will make you healthy, wealthy and (adjective)." Then she holds out a (noun) for you to take which makes you feel (feeling). You (verb) your teacher and turn back to your (adjective) path. The road seems so much more (adjective) on your way home. You emerge from the (noun) into bright (adjective) light, feeling (verb, past tense) and (verb, past tense).

When you are ready slowly open your (body part) and return to this (noun).

91

Numerology to Find the Inner Fool

To know ourselves even better, here is numerology to find our inner selves. Using your full birth name, pull out the vowels. Using the following chart, total the values of all the vowels. If you get a two digit number, add those together until you end up with one digit (for example, 9+6 = 15, 1+5=6, your one digit number). This is the number that is most truly you!

A=1
E=5
I=9
O=6
U=3

Read aloud the following interpretations:

1.

You have a personality as strong as limburger cheese. You want to be in charge. It doesn't matter what you are in charge of – the US Senate or taking out the garbage (aren't they the same thing?). If you can't be the top dog and have things your own way you will be miserable, troubled, unfulfilled and inclined to throw fits in Wal-Mart. You are tremendously independent, and if anyone gets in your way you may just trample them with your LL Bean boots.

2.

What a marshmallow! Your theme song is, "love me, love me, walk all over me." (you may be a perfect co-dependent match for #1.) You want to be loved, appreciated, cared for and live in a world of peace and harmony. You may seem unmotivated and unassertive, inclined to be a follower. Well, just be sure to ask where the person you are following is headed. Wake up and smell the de-caf! It may be time for some assertiveness training.

3.
Party down, dudette! You want to live in a bright bubble full of pleasure, surrounded by all that is beautiful, glamorous and entertaining. You want to make a splash wearing lamé & jewels. You are good-natured, affectionate and inclined to talk a mile-a-minute. Consider joining a major corporation for subversive purposes. You can always wear lamé petticoats under that pin-striped suit.

4.
Your hearts' desire is to get serious and get the work done. Foo on frivolity, you say. Accomplish, accomplish, accomplish is your watchword: structure and disclipine is the way to do it. Whoa there, kid. Lighten up! Before you box yourself in, realize there's magic all around. Go out to the supermarket at 3 am and get some Ben & Jerry's New York Superfudge Chunk and watch "Killer Tomatoes on Mars." It may change your whole per-spective.

5.
You don't want to be hemmed in or tied down (except maybe occasionally by a tall, dark, handsome stranger). You want to tear off in many directions at once and have an urge for travel, new places and new faces. Routine and monotony drive you crazy. You are the kind who will go down to the corner store for a package of twinkies and come back five years later. No doubt you are partners with a 4.

6.

You want to be part of a loving group. Because you willingly take on responsibilities and problems, people are always dumping on you. You are the one who gets the calls at 3am (and I don't mean the invitations to eat Ben & Jerry's NYSFC and watch "Killer Tomatoes on Mars"). You expect the same love, sympathy and approval that you give others. Get real, woman! Turn the phone off at night.

7.

You possess a deep inner longing to separate from all the clutter, clang and chaos of everyday life and merge with boundless infinity. You have a thirst for wisdom, knowledge and mystery. You would be happy meditating and dreaming your life away. Now, if you just had a grant.

8.

You want all the marbles. You want authority, recognition and material success. You want to own a major corporation and won't allow your private life to interfere. Good thing you look swell in grey flannel. Once you have all the marbles, why don't you look for a mysterious 7 to support?

9.

You overflow with sisterly love and want to make the world a better place. You want to give yourself to so many things, people and causes at once, you may find yourself exhausted. You need to focus on one thing at a time. Since your heart's desire is to serve the whole world, just be sure you don't end up saying, "Will that be for here or to go?"

Releasing the Four Directions

Spirits of the East, the South, the West, the North,
We release you to your foolishness.
Let us return to the world of paying the bills and
changing the litterbox,
Keeping the spirit of the Fool alive within each of us.
We await your spontaneous return.

Singing

We recommend foolish songs

Opening the Circle

☆ Fairy Dust may be purchased at many specialty
or party stores. Any glitter will do.

Fuschia Bliss	Serenity Soundbite	Magic Wanda
Melody Windchime	Rave Review	Prosperity Birkenstock
Starchilde Spaceshot	Sunny Innerchild	Rainforest Crunch
Rune Stone	Cami Sutra	Cami Soul
Tala Tail	Lita Spark	Halcyon Daze
Dolphin Rolfing	Shiat Sue	Miss Tickle
Astral Travel	D.Cath Coffee	Isis Poodlefeather
Serenity Sundancer	Parsley Sagechild	Kali Flower
Rainbow Ricecake	Omega Fairywinkle	Inspiration Meadowlark
Amnesty Tiedye	Ann Chovy	Rosehip Delight
Aura Pixiestick	Aurora Borasall	Humility Earthmother
Eterna Smiley	Relentless Cheerio	Oma Dewdrop
Ultra Light	Perennial Starshine	Bonsai Bungeejumper
Happy Moody	Daffi Dill	Comet Cappuccino
Rowan Oar	Flotana Innertube	Waverly Wonderbread
Bitsy Bizarro	Jofu Oatbran	Celestial Stormsmoother
Eeda Honeybear	Random Access	Waterlily Joyseeker
Sunflower Starhopper	Luna Sea	Lavender Nightshade

Rituals to Celebrate Personal Milestones

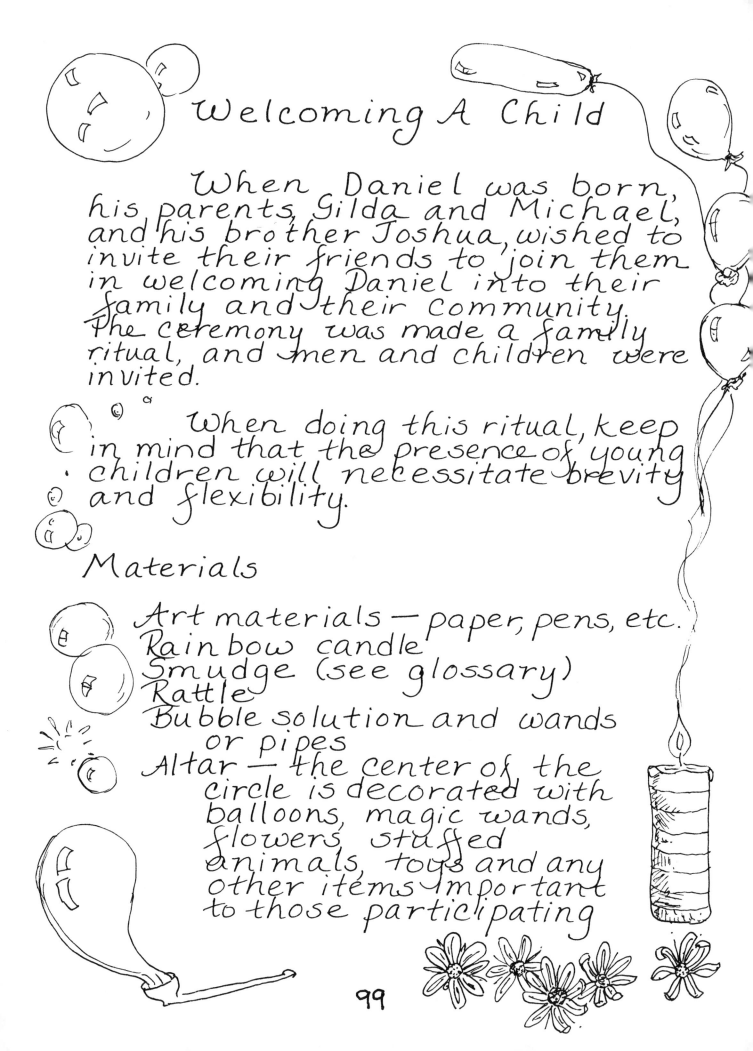

Welcoming A Child

When Daniel was born, his parents, Gilda and Michael, and his brother Joshua, wished to invite their friends to join them in welcoming Daniel into their family and their community. The ceremony was made a family ritual, and men and children were invited.

When doing this ritual, keep in mind that the presence of young children will necessitate brevity and flexibility.

Materials

Art materials — paper, pens, etc.
Rainbow candle
Smudge (see glossary)
Rattle
Bubble solution and wands or pipes
Altar — the center of the circle is decorated with balloons, magic wands, flowers, stuffed animals, toys and any other items important to those participating

Suggested poetry readings:
"On Children," from _The Prophet_, by Kahlil Gibran*
and _The Way to Start a Day_, by Byrd Baylor**

Casting the Circle

In addition to the usual candles, include a rainbow candle for the child being welcomed.

Family members may help in the creation of sacred space by offering smudge smoke to the Four Directions, to Earth and to Sky, and circling the space with a rattle (especially good for an older sibling to do).

Welcoming

Start by sharing some active children's games to encourage participation and to remind everyone of the wonderful lack of inhibition in a child's play.

After a brief quiet time to settle the energy again, break into small groups and discuss the following questions:

100

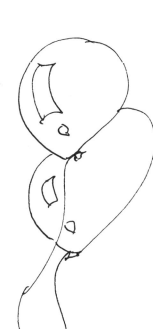

1) Whom do I define as my "family?"

2) What is special about my circle of family and friends?

3) What gift will I give this child and all the children who live in this world?

Gifts

Individually, create a gift for the child with the art gift materials.

The family then stands in the center of the circle and those present offer their gifts: poetry, stories, good wishes, any gifts just created.

Marilyn Robb offered this blessing to Daniel:

Our children are not our children
They are arrows from the past sent to the future
Like us, they are called, and they must go.***

101

We, as a community, enjoy a special bond with Daniel as a result of this night.

We enjoy a bond and share a responsibility to be a community to care for Daniel and Gilda, Michael and Joshua.

— a community helping to create a safe world for Daniel to grow into
— a community joining Gilda, Michael and Joshua in teaching Daniel how to be a full and rightly alive man
— a community learning from Daniel as well

Go on your way to a new and expanded life — growing and giving, seeking and receiving.

Bonded tonight, we fly as arrows on our sent paths — alone, together, side-by-side — with our own feather colors, our own special gifts, encircling this family and this new life in Daniel, and hence, in all of us.

Thank you, Gilda, Michael and Joshua, for sharing Daniel with us, for sharing your lives with us all. May the peace and blessing of the always-creating Goddess be with you all.

Blessed be. Ho.

Opening the Circle

Close with singing and blowing bubbles. Star shaped cookies and cider make a nice ceremonial feast. "May the star of hope be in us always." ****

* Kahlil Gibran, "On Children" from The Prophet, set to music by Ysaye M. Barnwell, Barnwell Notes Co., 1980, and recorded by Sweet Honey in the Rock on Good News (Chicago, Flying Fish Records, 1981).

** Byrd Baylor, The Way to Start A Day (New York, Aladdin Books, 1986).

*** From a song by Dorrie Ellzey, Ecumenical Women's Centers, 1653 W. School St., Chicago, IL, paraphrasing Kahlil Gibran.

**** Starhawk, The Spiral Dance (San Francisco, Harper & Row, 1979), p. 179.

NAMING

Many women rename themselves. Some take names that only they know. Some share these names only within spiritual gatherings and sacred space, and some use their new name(s) every day. Some women simply begin using a new name and some legalize their choice.

This ceremony is about honoring that choice and about bringing it into one's life in a ritual way.

The ritual is led by the woman changing her name. Unlike a surprise birthday party, your ritual will be most effective if planned by you for yourself, with others sharing in the planning rather than planning it for you.

When you start to plan your ritual, remember that it's okay to call this much attention to yourself. You're worth it! Reaffirm this any time you need to.

MATERIALS

Four Directions Candles

Bowl of salt water

Small white stones — placed in the salt water before the ritual begins, at least one for each person attending the ritual

Small black stones — to be added to the bowl of salt water later, at least one for each person

MAAT · METIS · TUFU · IRIS · I · MAY · NIMUË · PHOEBE · SELENE · YEMANJA · OSHUN · SAPPHO · AMATERASU · SEKHMET · LI · CAROL · MARGE · MALENE · ANNA · SHEKINAH · AUTUM · LEVANAH · WHITE BUFFALO WOMAN · SCORPIA · PRITHIVI · NUIT · SUSANI · CORN · SOPHIA · SEAR · P · AU SET · LI · ITH · ECLIPSE · YEMANJA · PITI · MAWU · BRANWEN · NEPHTYS · PASIPHAE · TIAMET · RHADIA · THCEIA · ARINNA · MAIRES · ATHENA · MNEMOSYNE · ROBIN · CYTHERIA · HATHOR · FREIA · JUNO · ANATH · ISHTAR · E · HEBE · HECEIR · MARIANNE · HWEDO · SEMELE · AIDONE · BETONY · THEMIS · RHEA · EURYDICE · BELTIS · ASHERAH · RAVEN · MORRIGAN · LOBA · EURYNOME · URANIA · BRIZO · CRYSTAL WOMAN · CRONE · RAINBOW · EAGLE WOMAN · JULIA · HABONDIA · HELEN · FRACE · R ·

Flowers

Gifts — on the altar or nearby

Anything else that represents who you are and who you are becoming

FACE PAINTING

The naming ritual begins as people arrive. Face painting is a good way to create a festive mood and get conversations going. There are several brands of watercolor crayons, such as Caran d'Ache, that are non-irritating to the skin. Those attending draw symbols, colors, simple patterns on their own faces or let others draw for them.

CASTING THE CIRCLE

Invite the energies of the Four Directions, lighting candles for each and naming the direction's current significance in your life. Each woman in the circle names herself, then joins hands with the next woman.

STORYTELLING

Tell the story of how you came to choose your new name.

LETTING GO AND HOLDING ON

Talk about how the name(s) you are letting go of has been significant to you — its origins, who named you, etc.

Place a black stone in the bowl of salt water to represent what you let go of in letting go of the name. Take a white stone from the bowl to represent what you wish to hold onto in memories and strengths of the old name(s).

Pass around the bowl and the black stones and ask each person to drop in a black stone for letting go of your former name and to take a white stone for remembrance. This is a time for others to share how you, your old name and your emergent name have been and are important to them.

GIFTS

Giving gifts to those who attend your naming ceremony is an option. You may want to give items that signify to you the change in your life. They can be different for each person or all the same.

This is also the time to receive any gifts others have brought for you.

OPENING THE CIRCLE

FEASTING

On all your favorite foods, naturally.

PARTNERSHIP

This ritual was created by two community members to celebrate their decision to share their lives with each other. It can be adapted to many forms of commitment. For this ritual, as with some others in this book, people other than regular community participants were invited to share in the celebration.

CASTING THE CIRCLE

In addition to the regular candles, light extra candles for those celebrating their commitments.

INTRODUCING THE RITUAL

This ritual recognizes that we live among our families and friends, not simply with one other person. It also challenges the expectation of the dominant society that a couple, whether or not legally married, is the only right, "serious" relationship.

INVOCATION

We come into the presence of the goddess, power of erotic love:
    in thanksgiving
    for women in community;
    for women and men who care passionately
    about life on this planet;

FOR ALL CREATURES, PLANTS AND ELEMENTS
WITH WHOM WE LIVE, MOVE AND HAVE OUR
BEING;
FOR OUR LOVE OF ONE ANOTHER AND THE
UNIVERSE.

WE COME INTO THE PRESENCE OF THE GODDESS,
POWER OF CREATIVE LOVE:
    IN COMMITMENT
    TO EACH OTHER AND TO ALL CREATURES AND
    ELEMENTS OF THE UNIVERSE.

WE COME INTO THE PRESENCE OF THE GODDESS,
POWER OF SUSTAINING LOVE:
    IN FRAILTY AND YEARNING
    TO BE CRADLED IN THE ARMS OF OUR FRIENDS,
    THIS COMMUNITY, THE UNIVERSE.

SONG: "HOLLOW OF MY HEART,"* SUNG BY ALL

MEDITATION

THIS MEDITATION HELPS US TO GATHER OUR
ENERGIES AND TO FEEL OUR CONNECTIONS TO ONE
ANOTHER AND TO ALL OF CREATION.

RELAX, ETC. . . . .

IMAGINE YOURSELF IN A FAVORITE OUTDOOR
SPOT. . . . SEE ITS COLORS . . . SMELL ITS FRAGRANCES . . .
FEEL ITS TEXTURES . . . HEAR ITS SOUNDS . . . . TASTE
ITS FLAVORS . . . BECOME PRESENT TO THIS PLACE. . . .

As you rest here, you gaze into a flower... deeper and deeper.... You can see into its petals, through its stem.... A ray of yellow light becomes a path for you to see still deeper and deeper... into the heart of the universe... into the presence of the goddess.... Look deeply... allow yourself to be open to the light.... Feel the light dissolving distance and boundaries.... Feel yourself becoming one, connected as with a lifeline... an umbilical cord to the universe.... Enjoy the love... the nurturing blood... the communion available to you..... Touch its strength ... its power....

(20 seconds)

The light drawing you into the universe now pours out and around all of us..... Our hands and arms fold into the light as we embrace one another .... Circles and spirals of light dance around us.... The light bathes the living things of the earth... deer and spiders, people of El Salvador and Russia, rocks and the very air itself.... We are sustained, the world is sustained by bands of golden love....

(30 seconds)

Gradually, the light fades..... The shapes and colors of the day return.... You become your separate self, and at the same time realize that you remain deeply, intimately bound with all of life.... Slowly, when you are ready, bring yourself back to this place... this circle... this room of friends.... this time of awakening commitment....

SONG: "WATERFALL," ** SUNG BY ALL

SHARING STORIES

THE WOMEN MAKING THEIR COVENANT SIT IN THE CENTER OF THE CIRCLE. THEY SHARE PHRASES, STORIES, IMAGES OF THEIR GROWING FRIENDSHIP AND LOVE WITH EACH OTHER AND WITH THE COMMUNITY. MEMBERS OF THE CIRCLE, AS THEY WISH, THEN ADD PHRASES, STORIES, IMAGES OF THE TWO WOMEN.

COMMITMENTS TO ONE ANOTHER AND TO THE FUTURE

THE TWO INVITE FAMILY AND SPECIAL FRIENDS TO JOIN THEM IN THE CENTER OF THE CIRCLE. THE TWO TAKE TURNS SPEAKING:

WE ARE HERE TO COVENANT WITH EACH OTHER, WITH YOU, OUR FRIENDS AND FAMILIES, AND WITH YOU, THIS BELOVED COMMUNITY.

WE HAVE CHOSEN TO BECOME A FAMILY, TO SHARE OUR LIVES, OUR STRUGGLES FOR JUSTICE AND OUR MATERIAL RESOURCES. BUT OUR COVENANT IS ALSO TO YOU TO LIVE IN THIS EXTENDED FAMILY AND COMMUNITY (THE SPEAKER POINTS TO THE SMALL CIRCLE OF FRIENDS AND FAMILY AND THEN TO THE LARGER CIRCLE).

WILL YOU BE OUR EXTENDED FAMILY AND COMMUNITY? WILL YOU BE A SPECIAL PART OF THAT YELLOW LIGHT HOLDING US IN LOVE AND POWER? (SMALL AND LARGE CIRCLES RESPOND AS MOVED...)

AND WE WILL HOLD YOU. TOGETHER, WE WILL LEARN TO
TRUST THESE CIRCLES OF COMMITMENT TO ONE
ANOTHER, AND, STANDING SECURE IN THEM, BECOME
PART OF A SPIRAL JOINING US TO ALL OF LIFE.

ONE SAYS TO HER PARTNER:

————, I PROMISE
TO SUPPORT YOU IN EVERY WAY I CAN
TO BE FAITHFUL TO YOU — TO BE HERE FOR YOU
TO BE HONEST — TO BE MYSELF, SIMPLY ME
TO SHARE MY GIFTS, MY RESOURCES, MY TRAINING,
   MYSELF
TO BE GENITALLY MONOGAMOUS
TO WORK WITH YOU TO SUSTAIN THIS FAMILY
TO LOVE AND ENJOY YOU
TO CONTINUE THE STRUGGLE FOR JUSTICE IN THIS
   WORLD.

THE OTHER SAYS:

————, I PROMISE
TO BE HERE WHEN YOU HURT AND NEED ME
TO SHARE WITH YOU MY TALENTS, MY ANGER, MY SMILE
TO BRING MY TEARS AND MY LAUGHTER TO YOU
TO PLAY WITH YOU — AND TEACH YOU HOW TO PLAY
TO SHARE MONEY AND GOODS WITH YOU AND WITH
   THOSE WORKING FOR JUSTICE
TO BE FAITHFUL — HONEST AND WORTHY OF YOUR TRUST
TO BE GENITALLY MONOGAMOUS
TO WORK WITH YOU TO SUSTAIN THIS FAMILY
TO LOVE AND ENJOY YOU
TO CONTINUE THE STRUGGLE FOR JUSTICE IN THIS
   WORLD.

THEY EXCHANGE GIFTS EXPRESSING THEIR LOVE AND COMMITMENTS.

THE TWO WOMEN (ALTERNATING EACH LINE) THEN SAY TO THE SMALL CIRCLE OF FAMILY AND FRIENDS:

DEAR FRIENDS, WE PROMISE
TO BE HERE FOR YOU WHEN YOU NEED US
TO TURN TO YOU AND LET YOU SUSTAIN US
TO SHARE OUR HOME, MATERIAL RESOURCES AND GIFTS
   WITH YOU
TO LOVE AND ENJOY YOU
TO WORK WITH YOU IN THE STRUGGLE FOR JUSTICE.

THE CIRCLE (IN UNISON):

DEAR FRIENDS,
WE PROMISE . . .
(SAME AS ABOVE; MAKE HOME PLURAL)

THE TWO WOMEN (ALTERNATING EACH LINE) SAY TO THE LARGER CIRCLE:

BELOVED COMMUNITY,
WE PROMISE
TO BE HERE FOR YOU WHEN YOU NEED US
TO SHARE OUR HOME, OUR INCOME AND GIFTS WITH YOU
TO TURN TO YOU AND LET YOU SUSTAIN US
TO SERVE ON COMMITTEES AND PROJECTS
TO WITHDRAW ON OCCASION AS WE NEED TO
TO LOVE AND ENJOY YOU
TO WORK WITH YOU IN THE STRUGGLE FOR JUSTICE.

THE CIRCLE (IN UNISON):

BELOVED ————,
WE PROMISE
TO BE HERE FOR YOU WHEN YOU NEED US
TO SHARE OUR RESOURCES AND GIFTS WITH YOU
TO TURN TO YOU AND LET YOU SUSTAIN US
TO GIVE YOU SPACE AS YOU NEED IT
TO LOVE AND ENJOY YOU
TO WORK WITH YOU IN THE STRUGGLE FOR JUSTICE.

SINGING

OPENING THE CIRCLE

FEASTING

A FEAST OF CELEBRATION IS SHARED.

* WORDS AND MUSIC BY SUSAN SAVELL FROM
THE POWER OF MY LOVE FOR YOU, HEARTLIGHT
RECORDS, 1986.

** WORDS AND MUSIC BY CRIS WILLIAMSON, FROM
THE CHANGER AND THE CHANGED, OLIVIA RECORDS,
1983.

Letting Go

This ritual was designed to help us identify some of the burdens we each have acquired and to begin the process of letting go of those we no longer wish to carry.

Materials

Stones ~ at least one for each person, set in a pile or arranged around the edges of the altar

Basket or other container ~ large enough to hold all of the stones

Casting the Circle

Introducing the Ritual

As we live our lives we acquire a variety of feelings, issues, tasks, relationships, etc. that interfere with our being able to live as fully as we would like. Some of these burdens we have picked up on our own; others have been thrust upon us. Occasionally, what began as a chosen task may, over time, become a burden.

Since our lives are different, our burdens are different. We must each name our own burdens.

Visualization can empower us to do what needs to be done in transforming a burden. It can help us to identify a burden and, when the time is right, cut the thread that keeps us connected to it. If the bond is cut visually, then the physical letting go can be much easier. Seeing the connection broken is letting in the possibility for change.

Meditation

Putting Down the Stones

Relax, etc....

You are going on a walk. On this walk you will become aware of the burdens in your life, the weights you have picked up, taken on forgotten to let go of.

You will find ways to release yourself from these weights when they are not serving you well.

The day is warm... filled with sunshine and a balmy breeze. You set out for your walk feeling rested, your backpack on your back. As you walk briskly along a path in the woods, you begin to notice stones along the way. At first you pass them by as you admire the wildflowers and sunlight dancing on the trees....

(pause 15 seconds)

But eventually you slow down and you start to feel that the stones are in your way. You stop to pick one up. You look at it, touch it, notice its texture. How heavy is it? You decide to take it with you, and you put it in your knapsack.

As you resume your walk, you try to pay attention to the beautiful scenery but find that your attention is still on the stones that you are passing.

Along the way you pick up several more stones and put them in your knapsack. As you add each one you consider its meaning for you... its weight... its appearance....

(pause 15 seconds)

You are getting tired from the weight of your load. Your body is feeling tense. Notice where you are feeling the strain from carrying the stones. How does your body feel?

(pause 30 seconds)

You stop on the path. You consider turning back... but ahead you see a clearing and hear the sound of a waterfall. The hope of a chance to rest keeps you going. You arrive at the clearing and see a steep embankment. Below the embankment is a lovely, clear waterfall emptying into a lively pool, which empties into a stream that wanders off out of sight.

You are hot and tired from your walk, but you realize you cannot make it down the embankment with your knapsack full of stones.

The thought of descending the embankment is scary because it is very steep. You also begin to wonder how deep the water is. Again, you consider going back.

Finally, you take off your knapsack and, one-by-one, throw the stones over the embankment into the stream below. How different you feel without them!

(pause 15-30 seconds)

You leave your knapsack behind and begin to climb down.

You walk to the stream into which you threw your stones. You can see some of them there beneath the water. You smile at having gotten rid of them. Then you turn and walk away from them... upstream...to where the waterfall calls you....

116

When you reach the waterfall, you test the water in the pool and find that the temperature is perfect. You take off your clothes and immerse yourself in the pool. The water whirls around you like a gentle massage, and the sun shines on your upturned face.

(pause 15 seconds)

You are totally relaxed... you think about your walk, and you remember the stones that almost kept you from finding this haven. You think of the stones, one-by-one. You think of them being washed by the water, and you feel your anxieties being washed, bathed, calmed....

(pause 30 seconds)

When you are ready, leave the water. Dry yourself, find your clothes. Choose a different path back home. You feel refreshed ... cleansed....

As you walk back, you notice the changing colors of the leaves and recognize the changes you have experienced.

There are more stones on the path, but they are not in your way. You pass them by. How good you feel!

You have returned to where you began your walk. You are home... and you bring with you a new sense of freedom....

(pause 15 seconds)

When you are ready, return to the circle and open your eyes slowly....

117

Letting Go

After coming back from the meditation, remain in a circle. Invite each woman to choose a stone and place it in the basket in the center of the circle, naming what she is letting go of. Note: these stones should not be taken home ~ the intent is letting go, not acquiring. After the ritual the stones may be taken to a place of running water and deposited to be washed by the flow.

Having let go of all these burdens, it is time to draw in energy to replace that which you have given up. Open up to the energy of the universe and be aware that every molecule of air carries that energy .... The air we breathe has the energy of the universe ....Breathe deeply and take in the energy that is love ....

Singing

Opening the Circle

118

Ending A Partnership

This ritual was designed to bring closure to a relationship and to honor the transition to a new life. Originally celebrated alone, it has been adapted here for community participation.

If your community is an open group, you may want to do this ceremony privately, with friends or alone. If alone, you may want to ask someone to be nearby for support and sharing after you finish the ritual.

Materials

For the Four Directions:
    Crystals — Earth
    Incense — Air
    Black candle — Fire
    Small bowl of sea or salt water — Water
A number of small black stones
A larger bowl of sea or salt water to receive the black stones
A third bowl of sea or salt water with a number of small colored stones in it
Any items that represent what is being let go of and what is taking on new significance in your life

Clothing

Dress in something of significance to the relationship — your wedding dress, a piece of jewelry, something given to you by the other person. Have available a change of clothes, including something new that has been made, bought or given to you for this occasion.

Casting the Circle

Cast a protective circle with smudge smoke, incense, a rattle or bell or simply by walking around the room.

Calling in the Four Directions

Someone lights the black candle and says:
"I light this black candle to bring the fire of passion and determination to your letting go process."

Someone lights incense and says:
"I light this incense to encourage the air to blow the negativity and the hurt away from you."

Someone places crystals on the altar and says:
"I bring these crystals to let the earth reclaim any negative energy and transform it."

Someone sprinkles you with water from the small bowl and says:
"I bless you with this water to heal you and open your life to new possibilities."

The small bowl of water is placed on the altar.

Letting Go

Move into the center of the circle and share briefly with the group your purpose in doing this ritual.

Into the larger bowl of salt water place the black stones, one by one. With each, speak aloud those aspects of the relationship you wish to let go—any hurts, disappointments, guilts, fears. As you drop the stones into the water, transfer the energy of these feelings from your body into the stones.*

When you are finished, a member of the circle says:
"Take a moment to look within to be sure you have named everything you want to let go."

(Pause for any additions)

A member of the circle says:
"Let yourself see who you are becoming with this letting go. Envision what will be different, more fulfilling, more joyous."

Then, from the bowl of colored stones, select stones and speak aloud, one by one, those memories, feelings, enjoyments that you wish to keep.

Again, when you are finished, a member of the circle says:
"Look within, and be sure that you have named all that is important to you to keep."

(Pause for any additions)

When you are finished, stand and remove the garment that represents the creating of the partnership.

Say aloud:
"I am removing myself from this relationship.

"I am shedding the garment of this partnership to emerge newborn to whatever I choose to have in my life."

Put on your new clothes and recall your earlier vision of your transformed self. If you wish, share your vision with the circle.

The members of the circle sprinkle you with salt water from the small bowl to bless and welcome your emerging self.

Grounding:

Touch the ground or the floor and thank the earth for sharing her energy.

Opening the Circle

Thank the energies that have come to be with you.

Feasting:

* These stones may be taken outside and buried following the ritual. Since energy is neither negative nor positive, the stones do not become negative as a result of the absorbed energy. In returning to the earth the energy that is affecting us negatively, we are offering it for transformation.

After the ritual is an especially good time to have someone do a tarot reading to look at the new energies coming into your life.

HOME BLESSING

When two FSC members moved into a new apartment, they wanted to celebrate and consecrate their new home. They invited other Community members and friends to participate in this ritual.

MATERIALS

Bowl of salt water
Household items to represent the Four Directions, e.g.,
    East (air) ~ hand-held fan
    South (fire) ~ hurricane lamp
    West (water) ~ pitcher of water
    North (earth) ~ potting soil
Candles, one for each person
Sweet grass
Matches

CASTING THE CIRCLE

In place of the usual candles, light four candles for:

    Old friends
    New friends
    Those who will live here
    Those who do not have homes

INVOCATION

Hold up each of the objects representing a direction as the invocation for that direction is spoken. Someone reads:

123

East ~ "May the air bring freshness and clarity to
        each new morning."
South ~ "May the fire bring passion to each
        challenge throughout the day."
West ~ "May the water bring soothing and healing
        each evening."
North ~ "May the earth nurture growth and
        renewal each night."

CLEANSING

With the bowl of salt water, sprinkle each room
(including corners, closets, hallways, etc.), cleansing the
space of any accumulated negative energy. Invite those
present to participate in the cleansing.

MAKING SAFE

Sit or stand in a circle, hands joined. With eyes closed,
take several deep breaths in and out together, grounding
yourselves and focusing your energy.

One woman in the circle leads the others in a
visualization of enclosing the whole house in a bubble of
light, then bringing the light into the house and into each
room, creating a protected, safe space. *

BLESSINGS

Each woman is invited to light a candle and offer any
blessings or wishes she has for those who will live in this
space, including plants and animals.

When all have finished speaking, burn the sweet grass, fanning the smoke throughout the home to welcome clarity and well-being.

OPENING THE CIRCLE

FEASTING

* This visualization may also be done from the inside out, gathering the energy inside the home, circulating it through each room, then expanding it out through the walls to the rest of the world.

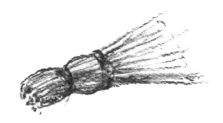

UNBINDING

These rituals help us to identify and release the messages that prevent us from claiming our own power. The first focuses on what binds each of us into powerlessness; the second focuses on the bonds of white privilege.

RITUAL I

Materials

Paper strips to make chains - colored contruction paper about 4" long

Glue, tape or staplers

Cauldron, epsom salts, rubbing alcohol (a mixture of epsom salts and rubbing alcohol will provide a small, safe fire)

Pens, pencils, crayons

Casting the Circle

Visualization

(Get comfortable but not too relaxed. This is a focused visualization, not a meditative journey.)

Sit comfortably, eyes closed. Take several deep breaths in ... out.... Let your attention focus on yourself ... on your breathing ...your body ...your own life.....

We all live with don'ts ... injunctions ... negative messages in our lives. Things we learn not to bring up ... not to do. . . .

Don't be articulate.
Don't speak your mind.
Don't make waves.
Don't be powerful.
Always think of others first.

And there are messages we hear that demean us — tapes we run over and over again in our own heads:

What makes you think you deserve help?
You can't do that!
Who do you think you are?
You never do anything right!

(Pause)

We are told we need to learn these <u>don'ts</u> for our own good — so we will know who we are and what to do! But often these <u>don'ts</u> bind us into submission and powerlessness:

Don't be too smart.
Don't compete.
Don't try to make it in a man's world.

As long as we live by these injunctions, while we buy them and abide by them, we can't and don't have to claim the power that is ours.

As you sit here in this circle, let yourself see the things in your life that bind you. What have you been taught or forced to accept? How has your life been shaped by these messages, these bindings?

(Pause)

Piece-by-piece, these "you-aren't-good-enoughs" build ... take on weight.... They bind your hands, your heart, your thoughts.... They bow your back.... They keep you from walking upright with your arms out to greet the morning....

See these words, these injunctions.

Acknowledge them, bring them into the circle with you so that we can work with them and release their power over you.... And when you are ready, open your eyes slowly....

Discussion (small or large groups)

What negative messages have you learned that bind you?
In what ways do they affect how you live your life?
In what ways do they affect other people as well as
    yourself?
What does defying these messages mean?

Breaking, Burning the Chains

Pass out narrow strips of paper. Everyone should have several. Each woman writes down what binds her and then connects the pieces to make her own chain.

128

All stand and form a circle.

One or more women move around the circle, fastening each woman's chains loosely around her wrists.

Light the cauldron fire in the center of the circle.

Begin to sing and chant:

> We can rise with the fire of freedom,
> Truth is the fire that burns our chains,
> And we can stop the fire of destruction,
> Healing is the fire running through our veins.*

During the singing, as they feel moved, women can begin to call out the binding messages they have written on their chains.

Let the energy build gradually from the singing into a single sound — a cone of power.** When the energy reaches a peak, the ritual leader calls 'Now!' and each woman breaks her chains. Move with the energy that has been created, making whatever sounds feel right.

Throw the broken pieces into the cauldron fire, releasing and transforming the energy.... As the fire burns, each woman reaches out with her unbound hands to the woman on either side of her, to form a circle.

Someone says:

"In breaking our individual bonds, we are able to reach out to our sisters and create a different kind of bond — one of support and strength."

Closing

Leave a few minutes at the end of the ritual for any further discussion necessary to complete the transformation of the energy. Ground the energy before opening the circle.

Singing

Opening the Circle

* Words and music by Starhawk, on the audio cassette <u>Chants</u>: <u>Ritual Music</u>, produced by the Reclaiming Collective, P.O. Box 14404, San Francisco, CA 94114.

** Starhawk, <u>Truth</u> <u>or</u> <u>Dare</u>: <u>Encounters</u> <u>with</u> <u>Power</u>, <u>Authority</u> <u>and</u> <u>Mystery</u> (San Francisco, 1987), Harper and Row, p. 108.

RITUAL II

Materials

Same materials as for Ritual I.

Casting the Circle

Introducing the Ritual

The theme of this ritual is racism and our responses to it as white women. The particular emphasis is white racism toward African-Americans. *

The note at the end of this ritual contains information which may be useful in introducing the ritual.

Visualization

Relax, etc. . . .

You are walking along a beach . . . it is a glorious day . . . windswept sky, deep blue ocean, dotted with whitecaps . . . .

You walk along . . . seeing the color . . . hearing waves . . . feeling the warmth of the sun on your body . . . .

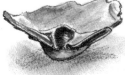

131

But your heart is troubled and tired. You work hard at home....

In addition, you may be in school, managing a job or career, doing justice work....

The pressures and responsibilities of your life run through your mind....

What are some of the images that come to you as you mull over current struggles and tasks...? How do you feel?

You walk along the beach, stopping to look at a stone, a shell, a sand dollar.... The day is warm around you....

As you walk on the sand, images of women come to you ... women of all colors and ages and shapes and sizes....

Women weave in and out of your mind and heart... carrying water... working in factories... nursing children... shooting dope... standing in unemployment lines... sleeping in abandoned buildings....

And you think of your own privilege....

You wish the sun would burn the images away, the waves would wash them out of your mind ... you have enough to deal with....

But the sun sweetly shines and the waves dance at your feet....

You stretch out on the beach, fitting the curves in the sand to the curves in your body...feeling the warmth beneath you...above you...feeling connected....

Can you allow yourself to feel connected to the women living around you, weaving in and out of your consciousness? What do those connections feel like...? Is there fear...guilt...longing...? Is there also distance...a gulf of alienation?

You begin to talk, to pray to the universe around you...to the universe flowing through the sun and sea and sand...flowing through the women...flowing through yourself...soaring through bones and cells and seaweed, through nerves and heart....

Who am I in this struggle to end privilege, you ask. Where do I fit in? You open yourself to receive answers, to struggle for clarity of insight....

(long pause - 2 minutes)

Softly, your prayer comes to a close. You trickle sand through your fingers in a gesture of benediction.... You arise and make your way back to daily life and this circle. (Allow some time for everyone to become present.)

Discussion

What is privilege?
How are you privileged because of your race?
How is your privilege connected with others'
     oppression?
How do your privileges bind you?
How can your privilege be used to create justice?

Breaking, Burning the Chains

Pass out narrow strips of paper. Each woman writes down the ways in which her privilege has bound her, limiting her experience, or ways in which her privilege has allowed injustice.

When all the chains are finished, all stand and form a circle. Each woman joins her chain to those of the women on either side of her, forming one large chain. Each lightly holds her section of the chain.

Someone says:

"We experience white privilege not just as individuals, but as a group. White privilege cannot be eliminated simply by breaking our individual chains; we must also do it as a group."

Light the cauldron fire in the center of the circle.

Begin to sing and chant:

We can rise with the fire of freedom,
Truth is the fire that burns our chains,
And we can stop the fire of destruction,
Healing is the fire running through our veins. **

During the singing, as they feel moved, women begin to call out the binding messages on their chains.

Let the energy build gradually from the singing into a single sound — a cone of power. *** When the energy reaches a peak, the ritual leader calls, "Now!" and each woman breaks her chains. Move with the energy that has been created, making whatever sounds feel right.

Throw the broken pieces into the cauldron fire, releasing and transforming the energy.... As the fire burns, each woman reaches out and takes the hand of the woman on each side of her to form a circle.

Someone says:

"In burning our chains we reach out to our sisters and create a new bond of equality and justice."

Song: "Singing for Our Lives" ****

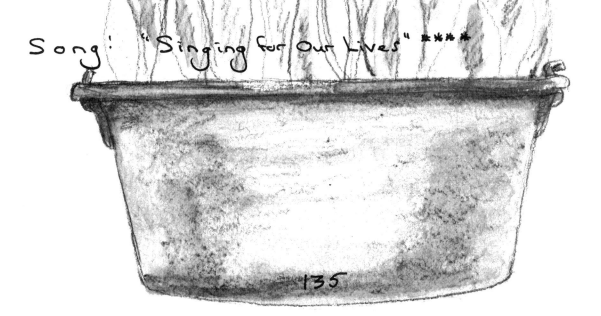

Closing

Leave some time for any discussion necessary to complete the transformation of the energy. Ground the energy before opening the circle.

Opening the Circle

* If you wish to explore white racism in relation to other groups, keep in mind that there will be both similarities and differences. Racial treatment of Native Americans is not interchangeable with the treatment of Blacks, for instance. The history of Native/white relationships is in many respects quite different from that of Black/white relationships. As a result, there will be differences in the way white privilege is expressed.

** Starhawk, <u>Chants</u>: <u>Ritual Music</u>, op. cit.

*** Starhawk, <u>Truth or Dare</u>: <u>Encounters with Power</u>, <u>Authority and Mystery</u>, op. cit., p. 108.

**** Words and music by Holly Near from the audio cassette <u>Singer in the Storm</u>, Chameleon Records, 1990.

Note

It is important to recognize that we live in a society whose social organization has historically been oppressive. Relationships, for the most part, have been based on a dominant/subordinate model (e.g. male/female, employer/ employee, teacher/student, white/Black). One group, or groups, has power over others and controls the lives of the subordinates. This model has meant that those underneath the dominants have much less social power to shape their lives, are dependent on dominants for access to society's resources, like food, shelter and education, and are threatened daily with violence, emotional and physical. Oppression is not simply the result of the action of individuals but has become systematized by society. Oppression has become pervasive throughout society.

The expression of oppression can take an active form — saying or doing something which has the result of interfering with the rights of an oppressed person or class. It can also be passive — doing nothing to change the status quo. The oppression can be either intentional — done consciously and justified by blaming the victim, or it can be unintentional — done without our awareness and justified by ignoring the victim. It is the consequences of the action or inaction which determine whether or not it is oppressive. (See the work of Robert W. Terry, Director, Education for Reflective Leadership Program, Hubert H. Humphrey Institute of Public Affairs, University of Minnesota.)

When oppression takes the form of racism, it can be expressed in three ways:

1) personal — done by individuals or groups of individuals. Whites who call Blacks demeaning names,

burn crosses or laugh at someone's telling of an ethnic joke express personal racism. Bigots are the most obvious example of racist individuals, although we all carry around racist stereotypes and feelings.

2) cultural - beliefs, values, scholarship that result in the inferior treatment of Blacks. Examples include beliefs that the white race is superior, more civilized; beliefs about the intellectual inferiority of Blacks; or images of Blacks as not fully human or ugly. These can be quite subtle and complex. For instance, a part of the myth of the dominant culture is that hard work leads to material success. Blacks are poor; therefore, they are lazy. Such a cultural belief ignores the history of the lack of access to decent paying jobs for African-Americans in this country and enables whites to feel superior and ignore the real causes of poverty.

3) institutional — policies, practices and power differences that exclude Blacks, impose special conditions on them, have special adverse effects on them. For instance, a "last hired, first fired" business policy may hurt Blacks more than whites because only recently has the business hired them. Having whites in management positions and Blacks in clerical or other supporting positions perpetuates pay income differences between Blacks and whites and prevents Blacks from helping to make decisions shaping our common future. Studying white history and culture and even African-American history and culture from a white perspective perpetuates ignorance, the sense that what white people do is more valuable than what others do and that whites are the final authority on culture.

All of these forms of racism also work to give privilege to whites. There is a level of trust accorded white people that Blacks must work very hard to earn. We are much less likely to be shadowed in a department store, have our gasoline credit card checked, be denied an apartment. We can be with other white people most of the time and in general work with, deal with white people — our people. We can see and hear white people and our own culture in stores and books, on the radio and TV. It may be largely male, but it's white. There are hundreds of ways in which white privilege shapes our lives every day.

If you want to read more about white privilege in daily life, write Peggy McIntosh for her article "White Privilege and Male Privilege" at the Center for Research on Women, Wellesley College, Wellesley, MA 02181.

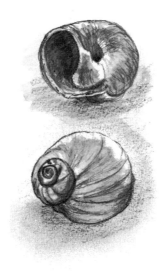

ULTIMATE VALUE

IMAGING THE SACRED IN OUR LIVES

This ritual was designed to celebrate the publication of, and themes from, Elly Haney's book, Vision and Struggle: Meditations on Feminist Spirituality and Politics. * It is not dependent, however, upon familiarity with the book.

It celebrates our experience of the sacred and helps us find images to represent that sacredness.

MATERIALS

Candle to honor ultimate value
Small candles, one for each person
Tape of slow, rhythmic instrumental music, to be
   played during meditation (suggested: Gabrielle
   Roth's Initiation ** tape)
Tape player

CASTING THE CIRCLE

In addition to the usual candles, light one for that which is of ultimate value in your lives.

INTRODUCING THE RITUAL

Each person on this earth experiences life differently. The events of our lives, our cultural heritage, our struggles, hopes and fears, our position in society all help shape our beliefs and values. In particular, they shape what is most important to us, who or what our "gods" are, what/who is of ultimate value.

Whether or not this belief is consciously identified,

we all have something which is our most important knowledge, something which is, to us, sacred.

When we talk about who or what is of ultimate value we use many images. The meditation and discussion in this ritual will help us find images that represent what is sacred in our lives. These images may be of god or goddess, a river flowing, a great spirit. In this ritual we will explore one particular image — that of the circle.

MEDITATION

This meditation is designed to be experienced standing (or at least sitting if 15-20 minutes of standing is uncomfortable). It is a physical as well as a mental journey. By moving to the music, your whole body will be engaged in the journey and available to experience sensations and images.

(Start background music playing. Play for 15-30 seconds before speaking.)

This meditation will take you on a journey to name that which is of ultimate value to you . . . to see how what is most important to you now has developed . . . to see how what is most important might have changed as you have traveled on your journey . . . to find images to represent that ultimate value . . . .

You are in a circle . . . you are part of the circle, you are the circle . . . . You reach out and take the hand of the woman who stands on each side of you and you feel the collective energies of these people who are this circle.

You breathe together, slowly, with these women . . . .

In . . . out . . . in . . . out . . . .

As you breathe with these women you realize you breathe with all of creation. You feel roots begin to travel down from your feet . . . into the ground, reaching down . . . down . . . drawing up energy from the earth, bringing it up through your legs, up your spine, up to your heart, out your arms and around the circle, sharing the energy, passing it out through your left hand and receiving with your right . . . . And you breathe with the earth and with these women . . . .

In . . . out . . . in . . . out . . . .

And you are relaxed and energized and ready for your journey . . . .

Your hands slowly drop to your sides . . . you remain part of the circle . . . within the circle . . . of the circle . . . and you know the sharing and strength is there . . . .

You are on a journey to name, to find images for, to see your gods or goddesses, what gives meaning to your life, what is of ultimate value to you . . . .

This is a journey of vision, of feeling, of hearing, of tasting, of touching . . . of moving . . . .

All of you is present . . . .

142

You begin to walk . . . . You find yourself moving, walking, as a child . . . a child in a world of discovery, coming to her first realization that there are ideas . . . images that represent to you how things can be and should be . . . a realization of what is important, what is sacred, precious . . . . You sense a time when some aspect of this ideal became conscious to you, even if you had no name for it . . . . However you can best know this time — through sight, hearing, taste, through touch, smell — you know that time now . . . . And you move with it if you need to . . . you speak it . . . you claim it . . . . You feel what is most important to this child-self of yours . . . .

(Pause 45 Seconds)

You move on . . . the images fade, change, are lost to hearing . . . . You move on to a time in early adulthood . . . . You've had many experiences now . . . . Your childhood has shaped you and you're ready to take on the world . . . to challenge . . . to claim your place in the world and in creation . . . . And you're sure you have all the answers . . . .

There are memories . . . ideas . . . images that come to you as you journey . . . . What is of ultimate value to you at this time? What is most important? What . . . whom . . . how . . . do you worship? What do you revere? Every sense you have is speaking to you . . . .

(Pause 15-20 seconds)

Is what is of ultimate value to you in young adulthood the same as what you knew was most important when you were a child? . . . . Is it a variation, a transformation of that knowledge? Is it completely different . . . ?

(Pause 45 seconds)

You move on . . . . You live, you choose, you learn . . . . And you are as you are now . . . . You have with you all of your memories . . . all of who you came to this ritual as . . . and there is no doubt about what gives meaning to your life now . . . . You see these things, and feel them and your mind can name them . . . .

(Pause 15 seconds)

Is what you now revere the same as what you knew was important when you were a child? A young adult? . . . Is it a variation . . . ? Completely different . . . ?

(Pause 45 seconds)

And now, you are here, in this room, in this circle . . . and you know the energies of those around you and you feel what is of value to each woman individually, and you feel what gives meaning to life within the circle . . . and with all of your senses you let the circle be a part of what is important . . . .

"To see the world, to see existence, to see Creation as circle is to see it no longer as an object for our use . . . . We are all together . . . all streaming from and toward the same source, the same possibilities, the same hopes and fears.
    "We are all bundled together . . . plant and animal . . . human and river and clay . . . not in misery and desperation and degradation . . . but in deep aquifers of love and justice and beauty . . . like seeds ready to blossom . . . loneliness to be healed . . . fear to be disarmed . . . . We are surrounded by grace . . . . We are pregnant with new birth . . . .

144

"Our vocation is to be lovers and beloveds . . . . It is to be in love with and responsible for the care and nurturance of the universe, including ourselves . . . . It is to delight in, be enchanted by, 'all things bright and beautiful.' It is to yearn for and know intimacy and communion with oneself . . . another person . . . a tree . . . the water . . . the kittens who live with us . . . the dolphins who live near us . . . . " * * *

(Pause 15 seconds)

We are here . . . we are this circle . . . and when each of us is ready . . . we will re-form the circle, sitting, letting our images come with us, taking time to reopen, refocus our eyes on this circle, these candles and these women . . . .

DISCUSSION (small or large groups)

What is of ultimate value to you?
In the meditation, what images came to you that represent what is of ultimate value?
Is the image of the circle helpful? In what ways?

CANDLES

If you have been in small groups, return to one larger circle. Each woman has the opportunity to light a candle and speaks of ultimate value in her life. Some may wish to light a candle without speaking.

CLOSING

All hold hands around the circle, eyes closed.

Someone reads:

"Again, feel the collective energies of these women who are this circle.... As you breathe with these women you breathe with all creation.... In... out... in... out.... Circling the energy....

Blessed Be...."

SINGING

OPENING THE CIRCLE

  * Elly Haney, <u>Vision and Struggle: Meditations on Feminist Spirituality and Politics.</u> (Portland, ME, Astarte Shell Press, 1989).
  ** Gabrielle Roth and The Mirrors, <u>Initiation</u>, Raven Recording, Red Bank, NJ, 1984.
  *** Elly Haney, op. cit., p. 88.

Rituals to Celebrate
Community

Storytelling

Storytelling can be done as part of any ritual, on any subject. This ritual is designed to encourage us to share our stories, specifically stories of our own spiritual journeys. It can be adapted to share other stories of our lives, e.g. those of becoming aware of being women; of racial, gender and other oppressions; of violence; of privilege; of solidarity with others.

It can also be adapted to hear other women's stories that have become important to us ~ to share readings of prose, poetry, art work created by others.

Materials

Talking stick (see glossary) or other object to be passed to each woman as she tells her story

Casting the Circle

Introducing the Ritual

Storytelling comes in many forms ~ writing, music, oral tellings, painting. Sometimes we tell ourselves stories in our dreams.

Telling our stories is creating ourselves ~ claiming ourselves, creating our communities. Our stories break silences and keep alive in the world those "dangerous memories and subjugated knowledges"* that those in power would rather we forget.

Meditation

Chakra Relaxation ✳ ✳

Sit or lie comfortably. Close your eyes. Take in a deep breath, slowly... deeply... hold it for just a second before you begin to release it just as slowly and completely....

Pause again at the depth of your exhaling. Then begin another slow taking in and letting out of your breath....

As you draw in your next breath, visualize or feel the color red coming in with the breath and draw the energy up only as far as your first chakra. Pull it up into your coccyx....

Breathe in again, drawing the red energy up as you inhale. Circle it around the lower spine, then exhale, allowing the tension stored in this area to flow down and out through your body.

Breathe deeply and draw orange energy up through you into your second chakra, your pelvis. Circle the energy around slowly, then exhale.

Continue with each chakra:

Yellow energy up into the abdomen....

Green up into the heart....

Blue up into the throat....

Indigo up into the forehead/third eye....

Violet into the crown chakra just above your head....

Breathe in deeply, draw the relaxation all the way up through your body, circle it throughout, and exhale slowly....

You are relaxed....

150

Meditation

In your relaxation you open your mind's eye and find yourself standing on a height of land. It's a wide, flat, safe height of land, with solid earth under your feet.

This height of land is your observation point. From here you can see, for a great distance in all directions, the country of your life...the landscape of your life....

You stand at your observation point and start to turn... slowly... looking around you. The sun will not be directly in your eyes at any time, so your vision will be clear... far-seeing....

There is a place in your life's landscape to which your attention is drawn... a moment... a time...an incident... a memory....

Though you may not have recognized it as such at the time, you now see that moment as a moment of change for you... a time when you began a spiritual journey...a journey that has led you here...to this group...to this community...to this room.... That moment of change may have been a revelatory, joyous event... it may have been an agonizing incident.... It may have seemed insignificant at the time....

You see that change... and you see it as the beginning of a river that has continued on since....

There are experiences you have had, decisions you have made since that have added to your river...branched into it....

What are some of those experiences or decisions?

(Pause 30 seconds)

How do they feel to you now as you look at them from your observation point? Did they lead you where you thought they would?

(Pause 15 seconds)

Your experiences have added to the river's twists and turns... its path.... You see the river flow at different rates as it travels over the changes in landscape... here it runs smoothly, quietly where the land is level... there it dips and races, tumbling down over a stretch of steep, sharp rocks....

(Pause 30 seconds)

You see all of that river as you stand on your height of land.... You see the flow of that first, important event carrying you to this room... to this community.... That event, that flow, is one of many, many that make up your story....

(Pause 15 seconds)

Gently, very gently, bring the knowledge of that time, the vision of that path, back with you now to this room... this group... this circle of storytellers....

And when you are ready... slowly open your eyes....

Storytelling (small or large groups)

Pass the talking stick, inviting each woman to tell the story of her spiritual journey. This is not discussion time — each woman speaks without being interrupted.

The following questions offer focus for the storytelling:

What was your moment of change?

How does that experience or decision feel now?

What has followed your decision that you didn't expect?

Where has your moment of change led you?

Closing

Song: "I Am a Strong Woman, I Am a Story Woman" * * *

Singing

Opening the Circle

* Sharon Welch, <u>Communities of Resistance and Solidarity,</u> <u>A Feminist Theology of Liberation</u>, (Maryknoll, New York, Orbis Books, 1985) pp. 32~54.

** With thanks to Nancy Grossman at Rowe Women Circles.

*** "I Am a Strong Woman" may be found on the audio cassette Chants: Ritual Music, produced by Reclaiming Community, P.O. Box 14404, San Francisco, CA 94114

Building Community

Communities need to be nurtured as well as the individuals in them. It is important to stop once in a while to acknowledge the role and power of the group and its collective process in our lives.

Materials

Feathers - one for each person, in a basket on the altar *

Small platform for the center of the circle, large enough and sturdy enough for a person to stand on

Drums and other rhythm instruments

Candle for the communities in your lives

Casting the Circle

In addition to the usual candles, light the candle for the communities in your lives.

Introducing the Ritual

We come together in communities for many reasons - to celebrate life passages, to accomplish a collective task, to dance, sing, be wild or quiet, tell our stories, laugh, touch and be touched.

154

IN THIS RITUAL WE WILL CELEBRATE THE CIRCLE OF STRENGTH AND SUPPORT THAT BUILDS FROM THE INDIVIDUAL'S PARTICIPATION IN COMMUNITY AND THE COMMUNITY'S RETURN OF THAT STRENGTH AND SUPPORT TO THE INDIVIDUAL.

EAGLE MEDITATION

RELAX, ETC. . . .

GO TO A SAFE AND FAVORITE OUTDOOR SPACE. . . . SEE THE COLORS AROUND YOU. . . SMELL THE FRAGRANCES ON THE AIR. . . HEAR THE NOISES OF THIS PLACE. . . .

AS YOU ARE RELAXING AND ENJOYING YOUR SPACE, YOU HEAR THE WHIRRR OF WINGS AND YOU LOOK AROUND. A HUGE EAGLE DRIFTS TOWARD YOU AND GENTLY SETTLES HERSELF ON THE GROUND BESIDE YOU. YOU SEE HER STRIKING WHITE HEAD AND THE BEAUTIFUL FEATHERS ON HER BODY.

AT FIRST YOU ARE STARTLED BUT SHE IS CALM BESIDE YOU. YOU RELAX AND REACH OUT AND SPEAK SOFTLY, INTRODUCING YOURSELF TO HER. . . . . SHE RESPONDS AND MOVES CLOSER. YOU CAREFULLY REACH OUT A HAND TO TOUCH HER BACK. SHE STANDS STILL, AND YOU STROKE HER FEATHERS. SHE INDICATES THAT THE TOUCH IS OKAY.

YOU REALIZE THAT SHE WANTS YOU TO CLIMB ONTO HER BACK. YOU STAND AND CAREFULLY PUT A LEG OVER HER. . . . . SHE WAITS FOR YOU, AND YOU RELAX ONTO HER AND CLASP SOME OF THE FEATHERS NEAR HER NECK. SHE MOVES HER WINGS SO THAT YOUR LEGS DO NOT HAMPER THEIR MOVEMENT.

THEN, SLOWLY. . . STRONGLY. . . EVENLY. . . SHE
RISES ON HER LEGS, SPREADS HER WINGS, AND
FLIES . . . UP. . . UP. . . .

AS YOU FEEL THE STRENGTH AND POWER OF HER,
YOU BEGIN TO RELAX AND ENJOY THE FLIGHT. . .
FEELING THE WIND. . . ENJOYING THE WARMTH OF
THE SUNSHINE. . . BRUSHING THE CLOUDS. . . . REACH
OUT AND TRY TO GRAB A PIECE OF CLOUD. . . .

TOGETHER YOU SOAR . . . AND GLIDE. . . AND DIP
. . . AND CIRCLE. . . HIGH OVER THE EARTH. . .
SKIMMING. . . PLAYING TAG WITH THE OCEAN WAVES

(PAUSE 1 MINUTE)

AS YOU GLIDE OVER THE WATER, A DOLPHIN
LEAPS UP AND YOU SOAR AWAY AND THEN CIRCLE AND
DIP BACK TOWARD THE WATER. THE DOLPHIN LEAPS
AGAIN AND YOU DODGE AND THEN DIP. . . . THE
DOLPHIN LEAPS YET AGAIN AND TOUCHES YOUR
OUTSTRETCHED HAND. . . . THEN THE THREE OF YOU
RACE— THE DOLPHIN SWIMMING AND LEAPING
THROUGH THE WATER, YOU AND THE EAGLE GLIDING
JUST ABOVE IT. . . .

(PAUSE 30 SECONDS)

AS YOU PLAY, YOU DECIDE TO SLIP OFF THE EAGLE'S
BACK. . . . STILL HOLDING HER FEATHERS WITH ONE
HAND, YOU FLY BESIDE HER. . . .

THEN YOU LET GO AND FLY ON YOUR OWN. . . .

YOU GLIDE ALONG THE TOP OF THE WATER, AND YOU DIVE DOWN AND SWIM BESIDE THE DOLPHIN, LEAPING AND DIVING WITH HER. . . . YOU SOAR UP OUT OF THE WATER AND FLY, YOU AND THE EAGLE DANCING IN SPONTANEOUS RHYTHM. . . WHIRLING . . . GLIDING . . . SOARING . . . CIRCLING. . . .

(PAUSE 30 SECONDS)

GRADUALLY YOU TIRE. . . AND CLIMB AGAIN ONTO THE EAGLE'S BACK. . . .

WITH HER GREAT POWER SHE CARRIES YOU BACK TO YOUR SAFE AND FAVORITE SPACE. . . . SHE LANDS GENTLY AND YOU CLIMB OFF. . . .

YOU THANK HER. . . . SHE NODS. . . AND FLIES AWAY. . . AND YOU RETURN TO THIS ROOM AS YOU ARE READY. . . .

A CIRCLE OF FEATHERS

THE RITUAL LEADER TAKES THE BASKET OF FEATHERS AND MOVES SLOWLY AROUND THE CIRCLE, GIVING ONE TO EACH WOMAN.

AS SHE GIVES EACH WOMAN A FEATHER, SHE SAYS:

"MAY YOU FLY WITH THE EAGLE THAT IS THIS COMMUNITY."

THE WOMAN REPLIES:

"I AM ___(NAME)___. I FLY WITH THE STRENGTH OF AN EAGLE."

157

THE WHOLE CIRCLE RESPONDS:

"FLY, (NAME) . FLY WITH THE EAGLE."

WHEN ALL HAVE FEATHERS, INVITE EACH WOMAN, AS SHE FEELS MOVED, TO STEP ONTO THE PLATFORM IN THE CENTER WITH HER FEATHER AND SHARE:

~ HOW SHE CAN BE AN EAGLE (BY OFFERING SUPPORT, LEADERSHIP, CHALLENGE, ETC.) TO SPECIFIC INDIVIDUALS IN THE COMMUNITY/OR TO THE WHOLE COMMUNITY; AND/OR

~ HOW SHE NEEDS THE COMMUNITY/TO BE AN EAGLE TO SUPPORT OR CHALLENGE HER.**

THE WOMEN OF THE CIRCLE USE THE DRUMS AND OTHER INSTRUMENTS TO HIGHLIGHT THE WOMAN'S WORDS, CALLING OUT ENCOURAGEMENT. WITH EACH WOMAN'S SHARING, THE ENERGY AND SUPPORT AND ENTHUSIASM BUILD. (NOTE: SOME WOMEN MAY NOT WANT TO STAND AND SPEAK, SOME MAY WANT A SECOND TURN AS TIME PERMITS).

SINGING

WHEN ALL HAVE HAD AN OPPORTUNITY TO SPEAK, STAND AND SING "WE ALL FLY LIKE EAGLES," "A RIVER OF BIRDS IN MIGRATION" AND OTHER SONGS. *** USE THE INSTRUMENTS AS ACCOMPANIMENT.

OPENING THE CIRCLE

* IF YOU LIVE IN THE COUNTRY OR NEAR THE OCEAN, MOLTED FEATHERS CAN BE COLLECTED NEAR BIRDS' NESTS OR GATHERING PLACES. IF YOU LIVE IN A CITY, THEY CAN BE PURCHASED AT CRAFT STORES.

** IN A CLOSED COMMUNITY GROUP, WHERE THE MEMBERS COME TO KNOW EACH OTHER BETTER THAN THEY MIGHT IN AN OPEN GROUP, YOU COULD BE MORE SPECIFIC ABOUT WHAT ONE INDIVIDUAL MIGHT OFFER TO ANOTHER OR HOW ONE COULD CHALLENGE ANOTHER TO FLY.

*** "WE ALL FLY LIKE EAGLES" IS ON THE AUDIO TAPE _GIFTS TO EACH OTHER: NATIVE AMERICAN CHANTS AND DRUM_, SUNG BY LYN MILUM. "A RIVER OF BIRDS IN MIGRATION" IS ON THE AUDIO TAPE _CASTING THE CIRCLE_ BY LIBANA, SPINNING RECORDS, 1986.

Room Blessing

This ritual was done November 30, 1981, as part of a celebration of our new meeting space. We honored the energies we brought to the room as well as the energies gathered by those who had been there before us.

Materials

Five candles — in addition to those usually lit

Container of rose water (see glossary)

Casting The Circle

Blessing Candles

Those who will light the candles stand in various places around the room. Each woman says one of these blessings:

I light this candle to create an atmosphere where we can safely draw upon our sources of power, trust and caring;

I light this candle to open the channels for our healing and supportive energies;

I light this candle to welcome the spirit guides who come here with us and those already here;

I light this candle to give
appreciation to the walls
that hear our voices, to the
floor that grounds us to the
earth, and to the ceiling that
protects us;
I light this candle to enfold
the diversity of the lives which
abound here.

Rosewater

A container of rosewater, symbol of
love and unity, is passed around.
Each woman sprinkles some to the
room, offering a blessing as she
sprinkles:
"In creating a safe space for
ourselves and all women, I bring
to this room COURAGE."
"... I bring to this room CLARITY."
"... I bring to this room JOY."
"... I bring to this room CHANGE."
"... I bring to this room LOVE."
"... I bring to this room LISTENING,"
etc.

Closing

When all have spoken, hold hands
around the circle, close your eyes
and share a minute or two of
silence to experience the gathered
energy.

Opening The Circle

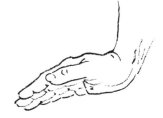

Healing Circles

Healing circles are times set aside to receive and/or give (channel) healing energy. They may be scheduled on a regular basis as well as requested whenever someone feels a need.

Materials

Green candle for healing.

Invocation

"I light this candle for the self-healing energies we each have within us. I call on the healing energies that are outside ourselves — energies that we sometimes need to draw on when we simply cannot find our own strengths within."

"I call on the power of the Mother, who offers color, warmth, love and blazing anger to encourage us to heal. May these energies come and be with us, and may we take memories of their healing ways home with us."

Casting the Circle

In addition to the regular candles, light the green candle for healing.

Introducing the Ritual

This century's medical "healthcare" models

have encouraged us (especially women) to turn over whatever physical problems we have to physicians for "cure" through treatments, or, more often, through use of medications.

But more and more we are reclaiming our bodies, our energies, our inner knowing. We are finding that by paying attention to what we feel within our bodies we can be in charge of our own healing, and that healing offered in community can strengthen the individual's process.

The healing circle is not one person "fixing" another. The healer draws energy down through her body and offers it through her hands. The healer does not take on the other's hurts or drain her own energies. Healing is shared by both.

Discussion (small or large groups)

Before doing a healing circle it can be helpful to talk about the nature of healing. We suggest that you select a few of the following questions and spend more than one meeting on the subject.

Questions

What is healing?
What is dis-ease?
How does healing happen and why?
What tells me that I am in need of healing?

What does being well feel like?
What do I imagine it would feel like?

From whom or what do I draw renewal and health?

How does energy move in my body?
How do I feel when the energy is blocked?

What heals me?
What nurtures me?
Are healing and nurturing the same?

Grounding and Centering
    (with all standing)

Eyes closed, hands relaxed at your sides, take several slow deep breaths in through your nose and out through your mouth. Imagine yourself having roots that extend from the base of your spine, down through your legs, out your feet and down into the earth. These roots anchor you and enable you to draw the earth's energy into your body as plants do....

Now, imagine a bright light of radiant energy above your head. It could be white or lavender or any color that feels healing to you. Open your crown chakra to this energy and see it filling you up and flowing over you like a waterfall.

Let the earth's energy and the radiant light energy become centered in your heart and balanced within you....

When you feel relaxed and centered, move quietly into the healing circle....

Healing Circle

Those needing healing lie in a circle with their feet facing the center, and the healers take their places around and between them. Healers place their hands directly on the bodies of those being healed.

Especially important areas are the head, the abdomen, the heart or any place identified as needing special attention. Energy can also be channeled with the hands above, but not touching, the body if this is more comfortable for either person.

For a minute or so after everyone is in place, healers should breathe in and out together, to let the energy settle and gather.

During the healing, the healers sing softly, tone, chant or remain silent. One person may quietly drum a heart beat. One healer should be designated Holder of the Focus.* This person will signal the end of the healing session by very quietly saying "Blessed Be."

Healing circles can run for varying lengths of time, depending on the depth and focus of the healing needed, but usually 15·20 minutes is enough. Beyond that, the healers' positions can become cramped, and it may become difficult to remain focused.

To close, withdraw contact slowly and softly, and bring your attention and energies back into yourselves. You may want to bend and touch the floor/earth to ground any excess energy. If time, energy and need permit, healers and receivers may change positions and repeat the healing.

The Holder of the Focus then suggests:

"Spend a few moments in silence to think of what you have felt and learned from the healing circle and what you have received. Send thanks to the universe."

Singing

Opening the Circle

* Gloria Romanic, <u>Women's Healing Circles</u>, (P.O. Box 22213, Barrie, Ontario, Canada, L4M 5R3, 1988) Soaring Hawk Enterprises, pp 54·55.

Notes

There is no RIGHT way to do a healing circle.

Keep in mind that what encourages healing in one person may feel uncomfortable to another.

Sometimes a particular person's energy may feel uncomfortable to you and you may need to ask that person not to work with you. Also, as a healer, you may choose not to work with a particular person.

It should always be okay for a person not to participate or to do self-healing instead.

While there are printed, visual and audio sources to help us answer questions about the nature of healing (see Resource List), when we give ourselves permission to look inside and pay attention to how we feel, we usually find that we already know the answers to these questions.

THE FIRES OF FEMALE FRIENDSHIP

When their relationship changed from being friends and lovers to one of "just friends", two Community members wanted to celebrate and validate this new form by ritualizing it. They decided to do the ritual at Community as a way of acknowledging that their friendship does not exist in isolation but, rather, is nurtured by and nurtures Community.

MATERIALS

Friendship candle, in a marbled pattern if possible. *
Objects for the altar special to this friendship.
"Sparking" candles — one for each person present and one extra. **
Basket of small stones — each with a flame drawn or painted on it, one for each person.
Matches.

CASTING THE CIRCLE

When all are seated, turn off all lights in the room. The two friends sit together at the altar. One uses a sparking candle to light the friendship candle, then the other says:

"From this sparking comes the flame of our friendship, a flame that we are here to celebrate, share and fan into new brightness with that sharing. We light this candle for the continuing joy and commitment of this and all women's friendships."

Continue with the usual lighting of candles, inviting women to bring the spirits of special women friends into the naming circle.

INTRODUCING THE RITUAL

We are celebrating our friendship for two reasons. One is personal: we are very important to each other, and we want to affirm that publicly and through ritual. The other reason is political: our society discounts friendship, and holds up marriage / partnership / sexual relationships as the most important and the only viable, permanent relationships between two adults. In particular, women's friendships are devalued, seen as trivial. In reality, women's friendships are:

- intimate — we reveal our real selves to each other.
- dangerous — we identify our common enemy and tell what we know.

169

- essential to life — they break our isolation, keep us connected to life; connection brings strength.

In her book <u>Gyn/Ecology</u>, Mary Daly talks about the "sparking" of women's friendships, of lighting fires "fueled by Fury", through which we love and encourage our own and one another's freedom. ***

STORYTELLING

The two friends sit in the center of the circle and tell the story of their friendship— how and where they met, what brought them together, their struggles as well as their joys.

THE COMMITMENT

They then make their pledges of friendship and commitment to each other, repeating the same words or using different pledges.

Each gives the other a token of her friendship.

RESPONSE FROM THE CIRCLE

The other women of the circle are invited to share stories about these women or observations about the friendship. They may offer support, wishes or even challenges.

THE SPARKING STONES

Pass around the basket of stones with the flames on them. Each woman takes one. One of the two friends says:

"These stones are a reminder of our friendship and also a reminder of the power and importance of all women's friendships."

PASSING THE FLAME

All stand in a circle, each woman holding a "sparking" candle. The two friends light their candles from the friendship candle. One turns to her left, the other to her right, lighting the candle of the woman beside her, and the flame of women's friendship is passed around the circle from one candle to the next.

When all the candles are lit, the women divide into two circles, one inside facing out, the outer circle facing in. Moving slowly in opposite directions, the women look each other in the eye as they meet, singing:

Listen, listen, listen to my heart's song,
Listen, listen, listen to my heart's song,
I will never forget you, I will never forsake you,
I will never forget you, I will never forsake you.****

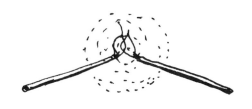

SINGING

"Dear Friends" and other songs

OPENING THE CIRCLE

* A marbled candle was chosen to evoke images of lives intertwined yet separate.

** Amscan, Inc. of Harrison, NY 10528 manufactures a package of eighteen 6¾" candles that sparkle as they burn. Party supply stores often carry them.

*** Mary Daly, <u>Gyn/Ecology</u> : <u>The Metaethics of Radical Feminism</u> (Boston : Beacon Press), 1978. See chapter 9, "Sparking: The Fire of Female Friendship," pp. 355-384.

**** This chant is attributed to Paramahansa Yogananda of the Self-Realization Fellowship and is recorded by On Wings of Song on their audio cassette <u>Many Blessings.</u>

SENDING

This ritual is a send-off for anyone going on a journey. The journey may be a temporary leave-taking or the beginning of a new life path in a new place. It was created in 1989 when Beth Koehler left to join the Women's Peace Convoy to Central America to deliver medical supplies and equipment.*

MATERIALS

Ribbons — three strands of ribbon, at least ½ yard for each person. The ribbon colors should be significant to the traveler and/or representative of her journey. One strand is for the traveler, one is for all who are her community and one for all whose lives will be touched by her journey

Two candles — one green, the other a color of the traveler's choosing

CASTING THE CIRCLE

INTRODUCING THE RITUAL

We are all on journeys and we each have a unique path. Each of us has something to offer the traveler, even if we have just met her. We have our wishes, our insights, our cautions and our encouragements to send with her as she begins a new time in her life.

STORYTELLING

The traveler tells her story of where she is going and why. Others who may have been there share stories of the place or of their involvement in the traveler's decision.

RIBBON CIRCLE

Three strands of ribbon are started together around the circle, each person in turn taking the entwined strands.

As the strands are passed, each person takes the end and expresses, either aloud or silently, what she wishes and hopes for the traveler. She then passes the ribbon on and the circle is eventually completed.

All of the group's wishes, love, hopes and energy have now been placed in the strands.

Scissors are passed and each woman is invited to cut out the section in front of her. These strands may be worn, set in a place of meditation, hung in a window to catch a breeze.

The ribbons represent each woman's connection with the traveler and her journey. As the strands are

174

cut, each woman takes the whole circle away with her. The circle is open but unbroken.

A green candle, representing harmony, balance, peace, growth and an open heart chakra is lit from a community candle and given to the traveler to light her journey.

The traveler may want to present a candle to the community to be lit in her absence.

SINGING

The energy of the singers' voices goes with the traveler as she journeys.

OPENING THE CIRCLE

* This ritual was adapted and used in June of 1991 when Diane Eiker went to El Salvador to visit our sister community of Guarjila, and in August of 1991 when Priscilla Skerry moved to Portland, Oregon to study naturopathic medicine.

METAMORPHOSIS

Accused of welfare fraud, Eddita Ocean Woman sought help from Community in dealing with the social systems she felt had failed her in her efforts to "follow the rules" of keeping herself and her children alive and sane.

Through the creation of an affinity group, formed as a nucleus of support, women of FSC worked with Eddita to identify her situation, her needs and her resources.* The support she received not only provided ways to deal with her legal situation, but also helped create the vision she needed to come through with strength and dignity.**

After her conviction and before her jail term, the affinity group and Eddita created this ritual as a way of reframing a situation of shame and powerlessness into one of empowerment and personal transformation.

MATERIALS

Candle ~ in a bright butterfly color, to symbolize metamorphosis
Drums and other rhythm instruments

BIRTHING CANAL (see glossary)

CASTING THE CIRCLE

In addition to the regular candles, the butterfly candle is lit for the power of growth and transformation.

INTRODUCING THE RITUAL

This ritual acknowledges the struggle in our lives that results from being members of an oppressed class (women and/or economically disadvantaged), and celebrates our capacity for change and self-empowerment. We will hear one woman's story and see how it relates to our lives, then go within to find for ourselves the place where change and renewal begin to rise out of those struggles.

STORYTELLING

Eddita begins by telling the story of how she came to be accused and convicted, identifying all of the "tapes" — the societal and family messages — that contributed to her diminished sense of worth and feelings of hopelessness.

As she tells her story, the women of the circle call out, in the voices of her accusers, the messages of her tapes:

"You're worthless."
"You're not supposed to feel sad, and especially not
        angry."
"You're not worthy of other people's care and attention."
"You're a failure as a mother."
"You have to fix whatever's wrong."
"You're weak. You need to be protected."
"You don't deserve anything better."
"Your family won't love you unless you're a good girl."
"You are alone."

Eddita concludes her story, saying, "Friday morning I will go to jail for two-and-a-half months because the systems do not work."

177

DISCUSSION

The circle breaks into small groups to discuss briefly experiences in dealing with systems that were oppressive and that seemed to hinder and/or judge more than to help.

Brigit reflects on Eddita's story and speaks of her movement from defeat and hopelessness to empowerment and courage as a journey of endarkenment, of going deep within to a place of change.

MEDITATION

Willow leads the meditation that takes us to our own individual places of endarkenment, places of gestation and silence. Places where change has not yet begun, but is about to....

Endarkenment

In recognizing where our individual struggles have been, we realize that we each have our own place within where change begins.

This meditation is a guided journey to take you within yourself, within a cocoon, within the silence, to feel that dark place in which change is nurtured.

Relax, etc....

Enter the journey of endarkenment....
The part of your journey that is like the dark of the moon... unseen.... It is the time of deepest night... where dreams dance.... It is the darkness that is the

178

silence of the universe before time began . . . before Grandmother Crone took the flame from the pocket of her dark cloak and flung the stars into the night . . . .

This is the journey of endarkenment . . . .
It is the time of the seed in the silence under the earth . . . waiting for the changes of warmth that bring new growth . . . .

This is the journey of endarkenment . . . .
The time of the unborn . . . floating in the waters of the womb . . . growing silently, waiting for the change to begin . . . waiting to move toward the light of birth . . . .

This is the journey of endarkenment . . . .
The time at the end of living as the body stills and the breath slows . . . and the spirit is midwifed through the darkness by the crone who guides the way . . . .

This is the journey of endarkenment . . . .
The darkness within the cocoon . . . where the caterpillar is becoming a butterfly . . . and new wings are spun . . . .

This is the journey of endarkenment . . . .
Where, in the silence and the darkness, we can find the flame within . . . the flame that is the gift of love and life . . .

This is the journey of endarkenment . . . .
Where we wait unseen . . . unseeing . . . like the new moon in the dark sky . . . knowing that this is the time of change . . . of metamorphosis . . . of love . . . of magic . . . the time of healing . . . .

(pause 30 seconds)

179

Soon, we will begin a new cycle of rebirth. . . . For now, we wait. . . .

(pause 15 seconds)

Let your mind come back, now. . . slowly. . . to this time . . . to this place. . . to this circle. . . .

And when you are ready. . . open your eyes. . . .

POEM (read by Eddita)

Metamorphosis

This morning I broke free
of my cocoon.
I thrust my head
into blinding white light,
sunlight.
It has taken some time
for my eyes to adjust.
Below me, waiting,
a field of yellow flowers
and sweet grass stretches as far
as I can see.
I am surprised.
Although I have been
struggling in the darkness
for weeks,
I did not know
how close I was to freedom.
I am resting now,
making myself clean,
shaking away the debris

of the cocoon
which confined me.
Soon, I will flex
my wings, extend them
and glide off
into fresh life
in this new world.

TRANSFORMING

Someone says:

"Eddita has found, through her experience, that the blaming messages of her life have hurt her. Rather than helping her to become a responsible adult, they have made her a victim. She is ready to transform the energy of those messages — ready to find her power."

Eddita and the women of the circle begin to call out, with stronger and stronger voices (accompanied by drums and instruments) the new words by which she wants to live her life:

"I am important."
"It's okay to feel sad and angry and to grieve."
"I am worthy of other people's care and attention."
"I am a success as a woman healing herself."
"I have friends who love and support me. I am _not_ alone."
"I am strong and do not need protection."
"If you don't get help the first time you ask for it, keep
        asking in different places until you get what you
        need."
"I am a strong and powerful woman."

Someone says:

"Eddita's process of transformation has begun.
Blessed be." * * *

SINGING

OPENING THE CIRCLE

* The affinity group model has been adopted and used several
  times since for special small-group support needs.

** Community's support of Eddita did not end when she went
   to jail. For the two months she was in the County jail, women
   organized visits, kept in touch with her children, kept track
   of her finances. When she was released, she was assisted
   through a cleansing and rebirthing ritual to complete her
   cycle of "going in and coming out" — to complete her
   transformation from hopelessness to empowerment and
   courage. We have included here more than our usual
   explanation of how a ritual developed because it is, to us,
   such an important example of how doing ritual in community
   __builds__ community and helps to reshape the world in which
   we live.

*** For more work with transforming negative societal tapes, see
    the Unbinding ritual.

GLOSSARY
✩
RESOURCES
✩
AFTERWORD

Glossary.

Birthing Canal   Two women stand facing each other and raise their arms to form an arch. Each two women who come through the arch stand beside the previous pair, raise their arms, and the canal forms into a circle as it curves and lengthens. After the last two women enter the canal, the first two join hands and travel through the tunnel single file, bringing the others with them, continuing on to form a circle as they emerge. All the while they chant/sing, "I am woman giving birth to myself....."

Effigy   Something created to represent a person, thing, idea, etc. In this case, the creation is then destroyed to signify the release of the influence of the person, thing or idea in one's life.

Grounding.   Earth energy is calming and stable. Grounding is making contact with the earth to center oneself, as well as touching the earth (or the floor) after a ritual to return excess energy.

Moonwater   Water in a bowl or uncovered jar left outside overnight to soak up the rays of the full moon.

Rosewater   Be creative. Add rose scent, perfume, fresh or dried rose petals to a bowl of water.

<u>Salt water</u>   Salt water is said to have cleansing properties. Use either ocean water or fresh water with seasalt to realign and clear the energies of healing stones or to perform blessings.

<u>Smudge</u>   Many spiritual traditions use the burning of herbs and/or spices to clear away unwanted energies and promote focusing and healing. In Native American traditions plants such as sage, cedar and sweet grass are commonly used, while lavender and sandalwood are common in European traditions.

<u>Talking stick, shell, stone, feather, candle</u> We're not sure of the origin of this practice, but in Native American traditions the talking stick identifies, during a gathering, who is speaking. In feminist process as well as in Native tradition, the person holding the talking stick speaks without being interrupted until she has said all she needs or wants to say. This allows full development of ideas and encourages others to listen. Everyone has a turn to speak.

~·~ RESOURCES ~·~

BABY BLESSING

Budapest, Zsuzsanna. The Grandmother of Time: A Woman's Book of Celebrations, Spells, and Sacred Objects for Every Month of the Year. (San Francisco: Harper & Row, 1989).

Stein, Diane. Casting The Circle: A Women's Book of Ritual. (Freedom, CA: The Crossing Press, 1990). pp. 145-150.

MENARCHE

Francia, Luisa. Dragontime: Magic and Mystery of Menstruation. Edited by Susun Weed. (Woodstock, NY: Ash Tree Publishing, 1991).

Kessel, Louise. "Goddess Stories," on audio tape. (PO Box 8, Bynum, NC 27228).

Loulan, Jo Ann; Lopez, Bonnie; Quackenbush, Marcia. Period. (Volcano, CA: Volcano Press, 1991).

Mariechild, Diane. Mother Wit: A Feminist Guide to Psychic Development. (Trumansburg, NY: The Crossing Press, 1981). p. 147.

Shuttle, Penelope and Peter Redgrove. The Wise Wound: The Myths, Realities and Meanings of Menstruation. (New York: R. Marek, 1986).

Stein, Diane. <u>Casting The Circle: A Women's Book of Ritual</u>. (Freedom, CA: The Crossing Press, 1990). pp. 150-156.

FORTIETH BIRTHDAY

Adler, Margot. <u>Drawing Down The Moon</u>. (Boston: Beacon Press, 1981).

Budapest, Zsuzsanna. <u>Grandmother Moon: Lunar Magic In Our Lives – Spells, Rituals, Goddesses, Legends, and Emotions Under the Moon</u>. (San Francisco: Harper & Row, 1991).

Mariechild, Diane. <u>Mother Wit: A Feminist Guide to Psychic Development</u>. (Trumansburg, NY: The Crossing Press, 1981). p. 134.

Rountree, Cathleen. <u>Coming Into Our Fullness: On Women Turning Forty</u>. (Freedom, CA: The Crossing Press, 1991).

MY BODY AS ART

Hutchinson, Marcia Germaine, Ed.D. <u>Transforming Body Image: Learning to Love the Body You Have</u>. (Freedom, CA: Crossing Press, 1985).

Newman, Lesléa. <u>Some Body to Love: A Guide to Loving the Body You Have</u>. (Chicago: Third Side Press, 1991).

MENOPAUSE

Beard, Mary; Curtis, Lindsay. Menopause and the Years Ahead. (Tucson, AZ: Fisher Books, 1991).

Boston Women's Collective. Ourselves, Growing Older. (New York, NY: Simon & Schuster, Inc.).

Costlow, Judy; Lopez, Maria Cristina; Tgub, Maria. Menopause, A Self Care Manual. (Santa Fe, NM: Santa Fe Health Education Project, 1989).

Hadditt, Marylou. Rights of Passage: A Celebration of Mid-Life and Menopause - A Play. (Penngrove, CA: PMZ Press, 1983).

Lark, Susan. The Menopause Self Help Book. (Berkeley, CA: Celestial Arts, 1990).

McCain, Marian Van Eyk. Transformation Through Menopause. (New York, NY: Gergin & Garvey, 1991).

Sachs, Judith. What Women Should Know About Menopause. (New York, NY: Bantam Doubleday Dell Publishing Group, Inc., 1991).

CRONING

Le Guin, Ursula K. "The Space Crone," Dancing at the Edge of the World: Thoughts on Words, Women, Places. (New York, NY: Gore Press, 1989).

Porcino, Jane. Growing Older, Getting Better: A Handbook for Women in the Second Half of Life. (New York, NY: The Continuum Publishing Co., 1991).

Rainbow (Sue Williams). "Croning at Pagoda". Broomstick: By, For and About Women Over Forty. Mar./April 1988, 10(2): 13.

Walker, Barbara G. The Crone: Woman of Age, Wisdom, and Power (San Francisco, CA: Harper & Row, 1985).

Ward, Edna, ed. Celebrating Ourselves: A Crone Ritual Book. (Portland, ME: Astarte Shell Press, 1992).

GRIEF, RAGE AND CELEBRATION

Adelman, Penina V. Miriam's Well: Rituals for Jewish Women Around the Year. (Fresh Meadows, NY: Biblio Press, second ed., 1990).

Bowman, Meg, comp. Memorial Services for Women. (San Jose, CA: Hot Flash Press, 1984).

Stein, Diane. Casting the Circle: A Women's Book of Ritual. (Freedom, CA: The Crossing Press, 1990). pp. 186-191.

CROSS-QUARTER DAYS

Ardinger, Barbara, Ph.D. A Woman's Book of Rituals & Celebrations. (San Rafael, CA: New World Library, 1992). pp. 123-174.

Pennick, Nigel. _The Pagan Book of Days._ (Rochester, VT: Destiny Books, 1992).

Walker, Barbara. _The Woman's Encyclopedia of Myths and Secrets._ (San Francisco: Harper and Row, 1983).

APRIL FOOLA

Ardinger Barbara, Ph.D. _A Woman's Book of Rituals & Celebrations._ (San Rafael, Ca: New World Library, 1992). pp. 113-116.

Hoffs, Tamar. _The Liberated Mother Goose._ (Millbrae, CA: Celestial Arts, 1974).

Musgrave, Kate. _Womb with Views: A Contradictionary of the English Language._ (Racine, WI: Mouther Courage Press, 1989).

WELCOMING A CHILD

Carson, Anne, ed. _Spiritual Parenting in the New Age._ (Freedom, CA: The Crossing Press, 1989).

PARTNERSHIP

Butler Betty, ed. _Ceremonies of the Heart: Celebrating Lesbian Unions._ (Seattle, WA: The Seal Press, 1990).

Perry, Deborah L. "Ancient Rituals Celebrate Women's Lives," New Directions for Women. 1986. 15 (6): 14.

Porter-Chase, Mary. Circle of Love: A Women's Unity Ritual. (Cotati, CA: Samary Press, 1987).

LETTING GO

Koller, Alice. An Unknown Woman: A Journey to Self-Discovery. (New York, NY: Bantam Books, 1982).

Mariechild, Diane. Mother Wit: A Feminist Guide to Psychic Development. (Freedom, CA: The Crossing Press, 1990). p.18.

ENDING A PARTNERSHIP

Stein, Diane. Casting the Circle: A Women's Book of Ritual. (Freedom, CA: The Crossing Press, 1990). pp. 209-212.

HOME BLESSING

Holmberg-Schwartz, Debbie. "Giving Each Other Our Blessings," Herizons. Winnipeg, March 1986. 4 (2): 4.

Mariechild, Diane. Mother Wit: A Feminist Guide to Psychic Development. (Trumansburg, NY: The Crossing Press, 1981). p.148.

Stein, Diane. Casting the Circle: A Women's Book of Ritual. (Freedom, CA: The Crossing Press, 1990). pp. 195-198.

ULTIMATE VALUE

Cantor, Dorothy W.; Bernay, Toni; with Stoess, Jean. Women In Power: The Secrets of Leadership. (New York, NY: Houghton Mifflin, Co., 1992).

Haney, Eleanor H. Vision & Struggle: Meditations on Feminist Spirituality and Politics. (Portland, ME: Astarte Shell Press, 1990).

BUILDING COMMUNITY

Bryant, Dorothy. The Kin of Ata Are Waiting For You. (Berkeley, CA: Ata Books, 1976).

Haney, Eleanor H. Vision and Struggle: Meditations on Feminist Spirituality and Politics. (Portland, ME: Astarte Shell Press, 1990). pp. 5-33.

Piercy, Marge. Woman On the Edge of Time. (New York, NY: Fawcett Crest, 1976).

Starhawk. Truth Or Dare: Encounters With Power, Authority and Mystery. (San Francisco, CA: Harper and Row, 1987). pp. 256-309.

Anderson, Sherry Ruth; Patricia Hopkins. The Feminine Face of God: The Unfolding of the Sacred in Women. (New York, NY: Bantam Books, 1991).

HEALING CIRCLES

Gardner, Kay. Sounding the Inner Landscape. (Stonington, ME: Caduceus Publications, 1990).

Mariechild, Diane. Mother Wit: A Feminist Guide to Psychic Development. (Trumansburg, NY: The Crossing Press, 1981). pp. 58-68.

Romanic, Gloria. Women's Healing Circles: Manual I. (Barrie, Ont: Soaring Hawk Enterprises, Box 22213 L4M 543, 1988).

Stein Diane. Stroking the Python: Women's Psychic Lives. (St. Paul, MN: Llewellyn Publications, 1988). pp. 147-174.

Stein, Diane. The Women's Book of Healing. (St. Paul, MN: Llewellyn Publications, 1987).

FIRES OF FEMALE FRIENDSHIPS

Daly, Mary. Gyn/Ecology: The Metaethics of Radical Feminism. (Boston, MA: Beacon Press, 1978). pp. 354-384.

Gearhart, Sally Miller. The Wanderground. (Boston, MA: Alyson Publications, Inc., 1979).

Hanscombe, Gillian E. Between Friends. (Boston, MA: Alyson Publications, Inc., 1982).

Hunt, Mary. Fierce Tenderness: A Feminist Theology of Friendship. (Crossroad Publishing Co., 1992).

GENERAL RESOURCES ON RITUAL

Austen, Hallie Inglehart. The Heart of the Goddess: Art, Myth and Meditation of the World's Sacred Feminine. (Berkeley, CA: Wingbow Press, 1990).

Beck, Renee; Metrick, Sydney Barbara. The Art of Ritual: A Guide to Creating and Performing Your Own Rituals for Growth and Change. (Berkeley, CA: Celestial Arts, 1990).

Budapest, Zsuzsanna. The Holy Book of Women's Mysteries: Feminist Witchcraft, Goddess Rituals, Spell Casting, and Other Womanly Arts. (Berkeley, CA: Wingbow Press, 1989).

Cunningham, Nancy Brady. Feeding the Spirit. (San Jose, CA: Resource Publications, 1988).

Eclipse. The Moon in Hand: A Mystical Passage. (Portland, ME: Astarte Shell Press, 1991).

Starhawk. The Spiral Dance: A Rebirth of the Ancient Religion of the Great Goddess. (San Francisco, CA: Harper and Row, 1989).

Starhawk. Truth or Dare: Encounters With Power, Authority, and Mystery. (San Francisco, CA: Harper and Row, 1987).

Stein, Diane. Casting the Circle: A Women's Book of Ritual. (Freedom, CA: The Crossing Press, 1990).

Stein, Diane, ed. <u>The Goddess Celebrates:</u> <u>An Anthology of Women's Rituals.</u> (Freedom, CA: The Crossing Press, 1991).

Stein, Diane. <u>Stroking the Python: Women's</u> <u>Psychic Lives.</u> (St. Paul, MN: Llewellyn Publications, 1988).

Stein, Diane. <u>The Women's Spirituality Book.</u> (St. Paul, MN: Llewellyn Publications, 1986).

Teish, Luisah. <u>Jambalaya: The Natural Woman's</u> <u>Book of Personal Charms and Practical</u> <u>Rituals.</u> (San Francisco, CA: Harper & Row, 1985).

Walker, Barbara. <u>Women's Rituals: A Sourcebook.</u> (San Francisco, CA: Harper and Row, 1990).

Walker, Barbara. <u>The Women's Encyclopedia</u> <u>of Myths and Secrets.</u> (San Francisco, CA: Harper and Row, 1983).

AFTERWORD

The weaving together of <u>Keep Simple Ceremonies</u> has affected every piece of our lives, especially our friendship. Mary Daly, in <u>Gyn/Ecology</u> (p. 368), said everything we could ever want to tell you about what the past three years have brought us:

"That was the beginning of our rough Voyage, which has proved — for those who have persisted — strange, difficult, unpredictable, terrifying, enraging, energizing, transforming, encouraging. For those who have persisted there is at least one certainty and perhaps only one: once we have understood this much, there is no turning back."

Diane and Sapphire
Portland, Maine
January, 1993

Sapphire   Diane

Diane is a new crone who has been a member of the Feminist Spiritual Community since her move to Maine from Minnesota in 1987. She is director of a child care center and has done teaching and workshops in the areas of human relations, early childhood education and non-sexist child care/parenting.

Sapphire is a registered nurse and has a particular interest in holistic health practices. She has done workshops on journal keeping for health and spiritual growth, and considers her discovery of the Feminist Spiritual Community in 1986 the best birthday present she ever gave herself.

Photography by Anne Koch and Roxanna Stilphen

More great Astarte Shell Press books for you to enjoy!

Please fill out or copy the form below and mail with check or money order payable in U.S. dollars to: Astarte Shell Press, P.O. Box 3648, Portland, ME 04104-3648, or call 207-828-1992 or **1-800-349-0841** to charge with MasterCard or Visa, or to request a copy of our catalog

Title	# copies	price	Total
Vision and Struggle	———	$10.95	———
Death by Crystal	———	8.95	———
Keep Simple Ceremonies	———	14.95	———
The Moon In Hand	———	12.95	———
Celebrating Ourselves	———	6.00	———
Anoqcou	———	6.50	———
Girl To Woman	———	10.95	———
The Rest of the Deer	———	14.95	———
Reflections of a Healing Heart	———	10.95	———
The Girl Who Swallowed the Moon	———	12.95	———
Women and Worship at Philippi	———	16.95	———
The Eighth of September	———	12.95	———
O Star (Sound Poem tape cassette)	———	9.95	———
		Sub-total	———

Maine residents add 6% sales tax ——————

Shipping costs: $2.50 for first book; .50 cents each additional book ——————

TOTAL ══════

Astarte Shell Press is a non-profit corporation, and is actively seeking grants, gifts and donations in order to continue and expand its mission to give voice to the voiceless.

Our logo is the Astarte shell, a small bivalve of the clam family found in the Atlantic off the coast of New England, where we live and work. The hand of the goddess Astarte is holding her symbol, the asp, which form the initials of the press.

NOTES

NOTES

NOTES

NOTES

NOTES